Daily Reading Comprehension

GRADE 1

Writing: Camille Liscinsky
Content Editing: Marilyn Evans
James Spears
Copy Editing: Carrie Gwynne
Art Direction: Cheryl Puckett
Cover Design: Cheryl Puckett
Illustration: Ann Iosa
Design/Production: Carolina Caird
Arynne Elfenbein
Yuki Meyer

EMC 3451

Evan-Moor®
EDUCATIONAL PUBLISHERS
Helping Children Learn since 1979

Visit
teaching-standards.com
to view a correlation
of this book.
This is a free service.

Correlated to State and Common Core State Standards

Congratulations on your purchase of some of the finest teaching materials in the world.

Photocopying the pages in this book is permitted for single-classroom use only. Making photocopies for additional classes or schools is prohibited.

For information about other Evan-Moor products, call 1-800-777-4362, fax 1-800-777-4332, or visit our Web site, www.evan-moor.com. Entire contents © 2010 EVAN-MOOR CORP. 18 Lower Ragsdale Drive, Monterey, CA 93940-5746. Printed in USA.

Contents

Week	Skills	Page
1	Comprehension: **Main Idea** Language Development: **Phonics** (initial consonant sounds, short *a*, rhyming words)	10
2	Comprehension: **Who and What** Language Development: **Sight Words** (*good, has, two, are, not*)	16
3	Comprehension: **Sequence** Language Development: **Word Meanings** (*water, bay, last, when, soft*)	22
4	Comprehension: **Compare and Contrast** Language Development: **Phonics** (rhyming words, final consonant sounds, long *i*, short *o*, long *e*)	28
5	Comprehension: **Fantasy and Reality** Language Development: **Sight Words** (*said, soon, ride, please, her*)	34
6	Comprehension: **Prediction** Language Development: **Word Meanings** (*dress, cluck, peep, grab, sticky, patted*)	40
7	Comprehension: **Main Idea** Language Development: **Phonics** (initial consonant sounds, final consonant sounds, long *e*)	46
8	Comprehension: **Who and What** Language Development: **Sight Words** (*then, use, his, put, eat*)	52
9	Comprehension: **Sequence** Language Development: **Word Meanings** (*bits, poking out, wiggly, when, hatch*)	58
10	Comprehension: **Compare and Contrast** Language Development: **Phonics** (hard and soft *c*, long *e*, long *i*, s/z sound)	64
11	Comprehension: **Fantasy and Reality** Language Development: **Sight Words** (*were, was, that, where, they*)	70
12	Comprehension: **Prediction** Language Development: **Word Meanings** (*spray, wavy, lacy, stack, meadow, everything*)	76
13	Comprehension: **Main Idea and Details** Language Development: **Phonics** (rhyming words, *oo*, consonant digraphs, long *e*)	82
14	Comprehension: **Who, What, and Where** Language Development: **Sight Words** (*under, could, went, must, live*)	88
15	Comprehension: **Sequence** Language Development: **Word Meanings** (*form, does, spill, breathe, dashed*)	94

Week	Skills	Page
16	Comprehension: **Compare and Contrast** Language Development: **Phonics** (compound words, rhyming words, *ou*, long *e*, *i* spelled *y*, short *a*)	100
17	Comprehension: **Fantasy and Reality** Language Development: **Sight Words** (*with, of, just, like, every*)	106
18	Comprehension: **Prediction** Language Development: **Word Meanings** (*jiggles, down, store, loaf, rumble*)	112
19	Comprehension: **Main Idea and Details** Language Development: **Phonics** (long *o*, silent *e* rule, hard and soft *g*, long *e*, rhyming words)	118
20	Comprehension: **Who, What, and Where** Language Development: **Sight Words** (*out, one, there, know, from*)	124
21	Comprehension: **Sequence** Language Development: **Word Meanings** (*set, bottom, pulled, jaw, pier*)	130
22	Comprehension: **Compare and Contrast** Language Development: **Phonics** (*oo/ou*, long vowels, *s/z* sound)	136
23	Comprehension: **Author's Purpose** Language Development: **Sight Words** (*over, through, let, white, have*)	142
24	Comprehension: **Prediction** Language Development: **Word Meanings** (verbs, *bumpy*, verbs, *wiggle, creaked*)	148
25	Comprehension: **Main Idea and Details** Language Development: **Phonics** (rhyming words, heteronyms, base words and endings, *s* blends, syllables)	154
26	Comprehension: **Who, What, Where, and When** Language Development: **Sight Words** (*saw, walk, after, this, old*)	160
27	Comprehension: **Sequence** Language Development: **Word Meanings** (*grader, toss, squirt, sprinkle, center, milk, kelp*)	166
28	Comprehension: **Compare and Contrast** Language Development: **Phonics** (*s* blends, plurals, syllables, *oo/ou*, long *e*)	172
29	Comprehension: **Author's Purpose** Language Development: **Sight Words** (*again, when, ask, eight, take*)	178
30	Comprehension: **Prediction** Language Development: **Word Meanings** (*shoos, change, trick, wag, chews, gnaws*)	184

What's in This Book?

Each week of *Daily Reading Comprehension* follows the same five-day format, helping to make the teaching and learning process simpler.

1. The weekly teacher page lists the skill that students will focus on for that week and provides a brief definition of the skill. Read the definition aloud to students each day before they complete the activities, or prompt students to define the skill themselves. You may also wish to reproduce the comprehension skill definitions on page 8 as a poster for your classroom.

2. The teacher page provides an instructional path for conducting each day's lesson and activities. Use the tips and suggestions in each day's lesson to present the skill and introduce the passage.

3. Use the student record sheet on page 9 to track student progress and to note which skills a student may need additional practice with.

4. Each student page begins with directions for reading the passage. These directions also serve as a way to establish a purpose for reading. Help students see the connection between setting a purpose for reading and improving their comprehension.

5. Because much of reading comprehension stems from a reader's background knowledge about a subject, take a moment to discuss the topic with students before reading a passage. Introduce unfamiliar phrases or concepts, and encourage students to ask questions about the topic. Also, as you read to your students, or as they read independently, help them see the connection between the words and the pictures.

6. After students have read a passage, a comprehension activity gives students an opportunity to practice the weekly comprehension skill. Questions are designed to look like the multiple-choice items found on state tests. Items use words and pictures to help students practice skills, whether or not they are fluent readers.

7. The comprehension activity is followed by a language development activity that practices skills in one of three important areas for improving literacy: phonics, sight words, and word meanings. The language development activity may be completed independently, in small groups, or as a whole group.

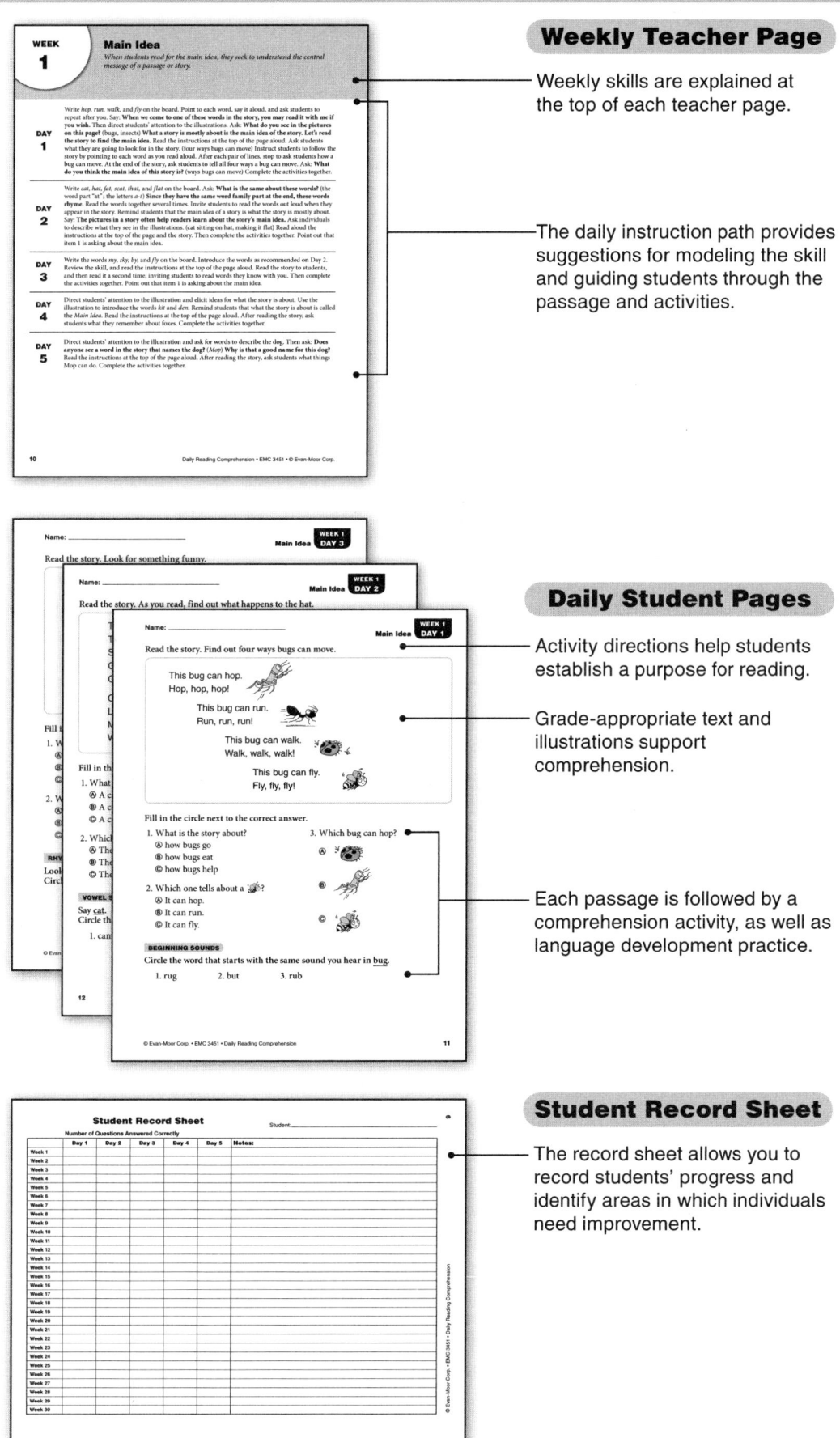

Weekly Teacher Page

- Weekly skills are explained at the top of each teacher page.

- The daily instruction path provides suggestions for modeling the skill and guiding students through the passage and activities.

Daily Student Pages

- Activity directions help students establish a purpose for reading.

- Grade-appropriate text and illustrations support comprehension.

- Each passage is followed by a comprehension activity, as well as language development practice.

Student Record Sheet

- The record sheet allows you to record students' progress and identify areas in which individuals need improvement.

Skills in Daily Reading Comprehension

Daily Reading Comprehension helps students become stronger readers by combining comprehension instruction and practice with language development. Every week, students are given the opportunity to practice standards-based comprehension skills, along with phonics, sight words, or vocabulary.

Comprehension

Students learn and practice six common comprehension skills that will help them become proficient readers and prepare them for reading assessments they will encounter in later grades. Each skill below is the focus of five weekly lessons, occurring every six weeks, for repeated practice and instruction:

- Main Idea and Details
- Who, What, Where, When
- Sequence
- Compare and Contrast
- Fantasy and Reality
- Prediction

Phonics

Gaining the ability to decode, or sound out, words is an important skill for becoming a fluent reader. The following phonics skills are practiced throughout *Daily Reading Comprehension*:

- rhyming words
- beginning and ending consonant sounds
- short and long vowel sounds
- digraphs
- blends

Sight Words

Sight words help students decode and read fluently. *Daily Reading Comprehension* activities focus on 50 of the 220 words from the Dolch sight word list:

after	has	not	saw	under
again	have	of	soon	use
are	her	old	take	walk
ask	his	one	that	was
could	just	out	then	went
eat	know	over	there	were
eight	let	please	they	when
every	like	put	this	where
from	live	ride	through	white
good	must	said	two	with

Word Meanings

Reading comprehension depends not only on being able to decode a word, but to understand its meaning. Each word meaning activity in *Daily Reading Comprehension* focuses on a grade-appropriate vocabulary word from that day's reading selection.

Scope and Sequence

	Comprehension Skills						Language Development Skills		
	Main Idea and Details	Who, What, Where, and When	Sequence	Compare and Contrast	Fantasy and Reality	Prediction	Phonics	Sight Words	Word Meanings
Week 1	•						•		
Week 2		•						•	
Week 3			•						•
Week 4				•			•		
Week 5					•			•	
Week 6						•			•
Week 7	•						•		
Week 8		•						•	
Week 9			•						•
Week 10				•			•		
Week 11					•			•	
Week 12						•			•
Week 13	•						•		
Week 14		•						•	
Week 15			•						•
Week 16				•			•		
Week 17					•			•	
Week 18						•			•
Week 19	•						•		
Week 20		•						•	
Week 21			•						•
Week 22				•			•		
Week 23					•			•	
Week 24						•			•
Week 25	•						•		
Week 26		•						•	
Week 27			•						•
Week 28				•			•		
Week 29					•			•	
Week 30						•			•

How to Be a Good Reader

Ask yourself these questions to help you understand what you read:

☐ **Main Idea and Details**
What is the story mostly about?
What tells me more about the main idea?

☐ **Who and What**
Who are the people in the story?
What animals are in the story?
What happens in the story?

☐ **Where and When**
Where does the story take place?
When does the story take place?

☐ **Sequence**
What happens first, next, and last?
What are the steps to do something?

☐ **Compare and Contrast**
How are two people or things the same?
How are two people or things different?

☐ **Fantasy and Reality**
Is it make-believe?
Could it happen in real life?

☐ **Prediction**
What will happen next?
What clues does the story give?
What do I know already that will help?

Student Record Sheet

Student: _____

Number of Questions Answered Correctly

	Day 1	Day 2	Day 3	Day 4	Day 5	Notes:
Week 1						
Week 2						
Week 3						
Week 4						
Week 5						
Week 6						
Week 7						
Week 8						
Week 9						
Week 10						
Week 11						
Week 12						
Week 13						
Week 14						
Week 15						
Week 16						
Week 17						
Week 18						
Week 19						
Week 20						
Week 21						
Week 22						
Week 23						
Week 24						
Week 25						
Week 26						
Week 27						
Week 28						
Week 29						
Week 30						

© Evan-Moor Corp. • EMC 3451 • Daily Reading Comprehension

WEEK 1

Main Idea

When students read for the main idea, they seek to understand the central message of a passage or story.

DAY 1

Write *hop, run, walk,* and *fly* on the board. Point to each word, say it aloud, and ask students to repeat after you. Say: **When we come to one of these words in the story, you may read it with me if you wish.** Then direct students' attention to the illustrations. Ask: **What do you see in the pictures on this page?** (bugs, insects) **What a story is mostly about is the main idea of the story. Let's read the story to find the main idea.** Read the instructions at the top of the page aloud. Ask students what they are going to look for in the story. (four ways bugs can move) Instruct students to follow the story by pointing to each word as you read aloud. After each pair of lines, stop to ask students how a bug can move. At the end of the story, ask students to tell all four ways a bug can move. Ask: **What do you think the main idea of this story is?** (ways bugs can move) Complete the activities together.

DAY 2

Write *cat, hat, fat, scat, that,* and *flat* on the board. Ask: **What is the same about these words?** (the word part "at"; the letters *a-t*) **Since they have the same word family part at the end, these words rhyme.** Read the words together several times. Invite students to read the words out loud when they appear in the story. Remind students that the main idea of a story is what the story is mostly about. Say: **The pictures in a story often help readers learn about the story's main idea.** Ask individuals to describe what they see in the illustrations. (cat sitting on hat, making it flat) Read aloud the instructions at the top of the page and the story. Then complete the activities together. Point out that item 1 is asking about the main idea.

DAY 3

Write the words *my, sky, by,* and *fly* on the board. Introduce the words as recommended on Day 2. Review the skill, and read the instructions at the top of the page aloud. Read the story to students, and then read it a second time, inviting students to read words they know with you. Then complete the activities together. Point out that item 1 is asking about the main idea.

DAY 4

Direct students' attention to the illustration and elicit ideas for what the story is about. Use the illustration to introduce the words *kit* and *den*. Remind students that what the story is about is called the *Main Idea*. Read the instructions at the top of the page aloud. After reading the story, ask students what they remember about foxes. Complete the activities together.

DAY 5

Direct students' attention to the illustration and ask for words to describe the dog. Then ask: **Does anyone see a word in the story that names the dog?** (*Mop*) **Why is that a good name for this dog?** Read the instructions at the top of the page aloud. After reading the story, ask students what things Mop can do. Complete the activities together.

Name: _____

Main Idea

Read the story. Find out four ways bugs can move.

This bug can hop.
Hop, hop, hop!

This bug can run.
Run, run, run!

This bug can walk.
Walk, walk, walk!

This bug can fly.
Fly, fly, fly!

Fill in the circle next to the correct answer.

1. What is the story about?
   Ⓐ how bugs go
   Ⓑ how bugs eat
   Ⓒ how bugs help

2. Which one tells about a 🐝?
   Ⓐ It can hop.
   Ⓑ It can run.
   Ⓒ It can fly.

3. Which bug can hop?
   Ⓐ
   Ⓑ
   Ⓒ

BEGINNING SOUNDS

Circle the word that starts with the same sound you hear in <u>bug</u>.

1. rug   2. but   3. rub

© Evan-Moor Corp. • EMC 3451 • Daily Reading Comprehension   11

Name: _____

Main Idea

WEEK 1 DAY 2

Read the story. As you read, find out what happens to the hat.

The cat is on my hat.
The cat is fat.
Scat, cat!
Get away!
Get away from my hat.

Oh, no!
Look at that!
My hat is flat.
What can I do about that?

Fill in the circle next to the correct answer.

1. What is the story about?
   Ⓐ A cat takes a hat.
   Ⓑ A cat eats a hat.
   Ⓒ A cat sits on a hat.

2. Which one tells about the 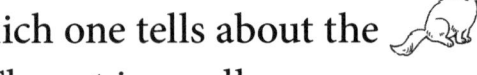 ?
   Ⓐ The cat is small.
   Ⓑ The cat is fat.
   Ⓒ The cat sits under the hat.

3. Which one tells about the hat?
   Ⓐ The hat is flat.
   Ⓑ The hat is fat.
   Ⓒ The hat is on the cat.

VOWEL SOUNDS

Say cat.
Circle the word that has the same vowel sound as cat.

1. came   2. all   3. have   4. play

Name: _____

WEEK 1
Main Idea DAY 3

Read the story. Look for something funny.

Oh, my!
I see a pig in the sky.
The pig is flying by!

A bug can fly.
A duck can fly in the sky.
Can a pig fly?

Oh, my!
A pig is in the sky.
That pig can fly!

Fill in the circle next to the correct answer.

1. What is the story about?
   Ⓐ A pig flies in the sky.
   Ⓑ A duck flies in the sky.
   Ⓒ A bug looks at the sky.

2. Which one tells about the pig?
   Ⓐ The pig is on a farm.
   Ⓑ The pig is in the sky.
   Ⓒ The pig is in a zoo.

3. Which words show surprise?
   Ⓐ flying by
   Ⓑ Oh, my!
   Ⓒ in the sky

RHYMING WORDS

Look back at the story.
Circle three words that rhyme with <u>by</u>.

Name: _____

Main Idea — WEEK 1, DAY 4

Read the story. Remember things about the foxes.

The mother fox is in a den.
The den is her home.
She lives with her babies.
A baby fox is called a kit.
The den is hard to see.
The kits are safe inside.
The mother fox feeds them milk.
She brings them meat.
She plays with the kits, too.
A den is a good home for kits.

Fill in the circle next to the correct answer.

1. Which one tells what the story is about?
   Ⓐ Baby foxes are small.
   Ⓑ Baby foxes live in a den.
   Ⓒ Baby foxes drink milk.

2. What is a **den**?
   Ⓐ the food a fox eats
   Ⓑ the name for a baby fox
   Ⓒ the home of a fox

3. What is a **kit**?
   Ⓐ a baby fox
   Ⓑ the home of a fox
   Ⓒ a mother fox

BEGINNING SOUNDS

Circle the word that starts with the same sound you hear in <u>fox</u>.

1. if   2. feed   3. puff   4. box   5. safe

Name: _____

Main Idea — **WEEK 1 DAY 5**

Read the story. Remember things Mop the dog can do.

Mop is my little dog.
He likes me best.
Mop hides.
I find him.
Mop jumps.
I catch him.
Mop plays in mud.
I wash him.
Mop sits on my lap.
I pet him.
Mop is my little dog.
I like him best.

Fill in the circle next to the correct answer.

1. What is the story about?
   Ⓐ a girl and her dog
   Ⓑ a dog and a boy
   Ⓒ a big dog who hides

2. Which one tells about Mop?
   Ⓐ Mop is a little cat.
   Ⓑ Mop is a big dog.
   Ⓒ Mop is a little dog.

3. Which one tells about the girl?
   Ⓐ She plays in mud.
   Ⓑ She jumps.
   Ⓒ She likes her dog.

BEGINNING SOUNDS

Listen for the sound at the beginning of the word <u>man</u>.
Circle two words in the story that begin with that same sound.

WEEK 2

Who and What

Students read to determine "who" (the main character) and "what" (the main character's actions).

DAY 1

Direct students' attention to the illustration, and ask them to describe the pictures. (For example: The sun is making the pig hot.) Write any story words they mention *(sun, pig, hot)* and help students read the words. Read the instructions at the top of the page aloud. Say: **The main character in a story is the person or animal a story is mostly about. Let's read to see who the main character is and what that character is doing.** Ask students to follow along while you read aloud. Encourage them to read the words they know. Invite all students to read the words *Slosh! Slosh! Slosh!* After reading, ask students to tell the main character (a hot pig) and what the pig did (cool off by rolling in mud). Write the answers on the board. Then lead students in completing the activities on the page.

DAY 2

Remind students that a main character is the person or animal a story is mostly about. Direct students' attention to the illustration. Say: **Stories can have more than one main character. The picture on the page gives a clue that this story has two main characters. We are going to read about a girl named Kit and her dog.** Read aloud the instructions at the top of the page and then read the story. Ask students to follow along and read the words they know. After reading, ask students to show with their fingers how many main characters are in the story. (two) Write the main characters on the board. (Kit and her dog) Ask: **What is funny about Kit and her dog?** Then guide students in completing the first activity. End with the sight words activity. Ask students to read the sight words with a partner and then circle the two words that are the same.

DAY 3

Say: **Today's story is about fish called rays. Rays are the main characters of the story.** Use the illustration to identify rays and their fins that flap. Focus the students by reading the instructions at the top of the page. Instruct students to follow along and listen carefully as you read the story aloud. Stop while reading and ask questions. (For example: Why do rays flap their fins?) After reading, ask: **What did you learn about rays?** List facts on the board. Note if some students know additional facts. Then guide students in completing the first activity. Have students do the sight words activity with a partner.

DAY 4

Tell students that today's story takes place in a pet shop. Ask: **What animals are sold in pet shops?** If the suggestions are animals mentioned in the story, write them on the board. Guide students to read those words out loud. Then read the instructions at the top of the page aloud. Say: **We now know that the story is about a girl named Jen. As we read, decide what pet she will get.** After reading the story, ask for a show of hands as to who guessed that Jen would get a fish. Then ask students to say and complete this sentence: **The main character in this story is _____.** Complete the page together.

DAY 5

Direct students' attention to the illustration, and ask them to guess the main character of the story. (a dog) Read the instructions at the top of the page aloud. Say: **Let's find out about this dog. Follow along as I read the story.** Then reread the story, with students reading all the words they know. After reading, ask: **What is the name of the main character? What is the main character doing?** Guide students in completing the page.

Name: _____

Who and What WEEK 2 DAY 1

Read the story. Find out what the pig does to be cool.

The sun is hot.
It is too hot for the pig.
The pig wants to be cool.
It sees some mud.
Slosh! Slosh! Slosh!
The mud feels good.
The mud is not hot.
Roll, pig, roll!

Fill in the circle next to the correct answer.

1. The main character is _____.
   Ⓐ a pig
   Ⓑ some mud
   Ⓒ the sun

2. What does the pig do?
   Ⓐ The pig plays in the sun.
   Ⓑ The pig eats some mud.
   Ⓒ The pig rolls in mud.

3. Why does the pig go in the mud?
   Ⓐ The mud is hot.
   Ⓑ The mud is cool.
   Ⓒ The mud is messy.

SIGHT WORDS

Circle the word that correctly completes the sentence.

The mud makes the pig feel (got   good).

Name: _____   Who and What   **WEEK 2 DAY 2**

Read the story. Find out what is funny about Kit and her pet.

Kit is little.
But Kit has a very big dog.
So Kit has a very big room.
The room has one big bed.
And it has one little bed.
The room has one big toy box.
And it has one little toy box.
Kit is little.
But Kit has a very big dog.
Kit's very big room has very little room
    for Kit!

Fill in the circle next to the correct answer.

1. The story is about _____.
   Ⓐ a girl named Kit
   Ⓑ a dog named Kit
   Ⓒ Kit and her dog

2. Which one tells about Kit's dog?
   Ⓐ The dog is little.
   Ⓑ The dog is big.
   Ⓒ The dog sleeps in a box.

3. Which one tells about Kit?
   Ⓐ Kit has a little bed.
   Ⓑ Kit has a little room.
   Ⓒ Kit has a little dog.

SIGHT WORDS

Circle the two words that are the same.

1. had   2. hat   3. has   4. have   5. has

Name: _____

Who and What

WEEK 2 DAY 3

Read the story. See how many things you can remember about rays.

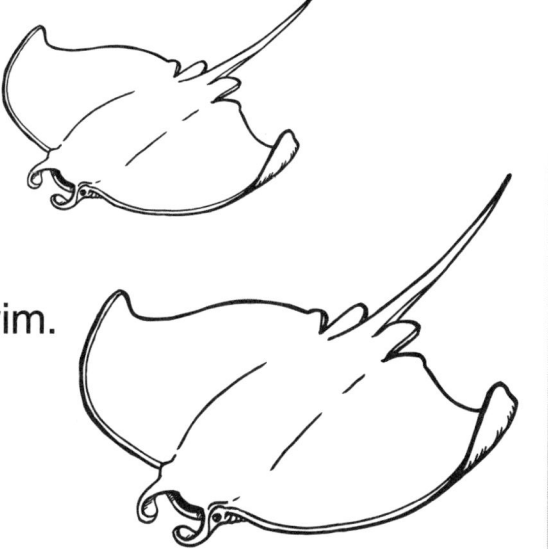

Rays are big fish in the sea.
They flap their two fins to swim.
Their fins go up and down.
They swim very fast.
Rays can flap right out of the water!
Rays open their mouths when they swim.
Their mouths are long.
Small fish go right in.
So rays eat while they swim.

Fill in the circle next to the correct answer.

1. The main characters are _____.
   Ⓐ small fish
   Ⓑ two fins
   Ⓒ rays

2. How do rays swim?
   Ⓐ Rays open their mouths.
   Ⓑ Rays flap their fins.
   Ⓒ Rays shake their tails.

3. How do rays eat?
   Ⓐ Rays open their mouths.
   Ⓑ Rays use their tails.
   Ⓒ Rays use their fins.

SIGHT WORDS

Circle the two words that are the same.

1. two   2. who   3. two   4. take   5. what

Name: _____

Who and What WEEK 2 DAY 4

Read the story. Decide what pet Jen will get.

> Jen is with her mom.
> They are at a pet shop.
> Jen can get a pet.
> She can pick the pet she likes.
> Jen looks and looks.
> The dogs bark too much.
> The cats sleep too much.
> The birds bite too much.
> The fish just swim.
> "A fish is best," says Jen.

Fill in the circle next to the correct answer.

1. Who is the story about?
   Ⓐ a mom named Jen
   Ⓑ a girl named Jen
   Ⓒ a pet named Jen

2. Why is Jen at the pet shop?
   Ⓐ Jen likes to feed the pets.
   Ⓑ Jen can get a pet.
   Ⓒ Jen's mom wants a pet.

3. What pet does Jen get?
   Ⓐ Jen gets a bird.
   Ⓑ Jen gets a cat.
   Ⓒ Jen gets a fish.

SIGHT WORDS

Circle the word that correctly completes the sentence.

Jen and her mom (is   are) at a pet shop.

Name: _____

Who and What   WEEK 2 DAY 5

Read the story. Find out what happens when a dog gets a bath.

> Rex stinks!
> He needs a bath.
> Dad puts Rex in the tub.
> Mom gets Rex wet.
> Rex is not happy.
> Dad rubs on some soap.
> Mom washes it off.
> Rex is not happy.
> Then Dad puts Rex on the floor.
> Rex shakes and shakes!
> Now Dad and Mom are wet.
> They are not happy!

Fill in the circle next to the correct answer.

1. The main character is _____.
   - Ⓐ Mom
   - Ⓑ Dad
   - Ⓒ Rex

2. Which one tells about Rex?
   - Ⓐ Rex is not happy in the tub.
   - Ⓑ Rex likes to get a bath.
   - Ⓒ Rex likes soap.

3. What happens to Mom and Dad?
   - Ⓐ Rex gets them wet.
   - Ⓑ Rex jumps on them.
   - Ⓒ Rex plays with them.

SIGHT WORDS

Circle the word that correctly completes the sentence.

Rex does (not   now) like to get a bath.

© Evan-Moor Corp. • EMC 3451 • Daily Reading Comprehension

WEEK 3

Sequence

Students practice Sequence to determine the order of events or steps in a process.

DAY 1

Tell students that this week they will be practicing a skill called *Sequence*. Say: **Sequence is the order in which you do something or the order in which things happen. Good readers look for signal words. Signal words are words that help readers understand the order in which things happen. As I read the story about growing a flower, listen and look for words that signal the steps.** Read the story aloud, and then guide students to circle the signal words *First, Next, Then,* and *Last.* Read the story again, encouraging students to read with you. Complete the first activity together, pointing out the signal word in each item. *(first, after, last)* Then read the word meanings activity. Say: **In order to do this activity, we need to read the sentence in the story that uses the word** *water.* Help students locate and read the sentence. Ask them to act out the sentence and then circle the picture that best shows what *water* means.

DAY 2

Remind students that *Sequence* is the order in which things happen. Signal words help readers understand the sequence of events. Review the signal words *first, next, then,* and *last* from Day 1. Direct students' attention to the story, and guide them to find and circle these signal words. Say: **Today we are going to read about two main characters named Jack and Cam. Use the circled words to help you understand the order in which things happen.** Read the instructions aloud, and then read the story while students follow along. After reading, ask half the class to read the four steps in finding the box while the other half acts out each step. Then guide students through the first activity by first circling the key words. *(first, last, after)* Read the word meanings activity. Say: **In order to do this activity, we need to read the sentence in the story that uses the word** *bay.* Help students locate and read the sentence. Encourage them to explain which answer is correct and why.

DAY 3

Remind students of the reading skill and ask them to give examples of signal words they have learned this week. Read the instructions at the top of the page aloud. Say: **Close your eyes while I read a story about a girl named Eva. Picture in your mind the steps she takes to open a present.** After reading, ask students to find and circle the signal words. Complete the activities together, pointing out the key words *next, after,* and *last* in the first activity.

DAY 4

Direct students' attention to the illustration and say that it is a drawing of a boy named Mike who is at a birthday party. Read the instructions at the top of the page aloud. Instruct students to raise their hands every time they hear a signal word. Read the story aloud. Then ask students to retell the story using the signal words *first, next, then,* and *finally*. Complete the first activity together. Guide students to find the key words in each question *(before, soon after, last)* before filling in the answer. Complete the word meanings activity together.

DAY 5

Ask students to use the illustration to determine the main character of the story. (a bird) Read the instructions aloud. Review what readers can do to help them remember the order in which things happen. (Circle the signal words.) Read the story aloud as students follow along. Ask them to tell a partner the four steps in building a nest, using the words *first, then, next,* and *last*. Complete the activities together.

Name: _____

Sequence **WEEK 3 DAY 1**

Read the story. Remember the steps to grow a flower.

> You can grow flowers.
> First, dig a hole.
> Next, put in some plant food.
> Put the flowering plant into the hole.
> Then, fill the hole with dirt.
> Pat down the dirt to hold the flower.
> Last, water the plant.
> Soon, the plant will grow flowers.

Fill in the circle next to the correct answer.

1. What is the first step to help a flower grow?
   Ⓐ dig a hole
   Ⓑ water the flower
   Ⓒ put plant food into the hole

2. What do you do next, after you dig a hole?
   Ⓐ water the flower
   Ⓑ put the plant into the hole
   Ⓒ put in some plant food

3. What is the last step to help a flower grow?
   Ⓐ water the plant
   Ⓑ fill the hole with dirt
   Ⓒ take the flower out of its pot

WORD MEANINGS

Circle the picture that tells what the word <u>water</u> means in the story.

1.    2.    3.

© Evan-Moor Corp. • EMC 3451 • Daily Reading Comprehension

Name: _____

Sequence   **WEEK 3 DAY 2**

Read the story. Think about the order in which things happen.

Jack and Cam want to find a box.
A map shows them what to do.
First, they row a boat across the bay.
Next, they walk one mile.
Then, they look for a red flag in the grass.
Last, they dig under the flag.
Cam and Jack find the box!
They look inside.
The box is full of gold.
"Cool!" says Cam.

Fill in the circle next to the correct answer.

1. What is the first thing Cam and Jack do to find the box?
   Ⓐ They row a boat.
   Ⓑ They walk a mile.
   Ⓒ They make a map.

2. What do Jack and Cam do last?
   Ⓐ They put a flag in the grass.
   Ⓑ They look for a flag in the grass.
   Ⓒ They dig under the flag in the grass.

3. What do Cam and Jack do after they row across the bay?
   Ⓐ They run a mile.
   Ⓑ They walk a mile.
   Ⓒ They row a mile.

WORD MEANINGS

Circle the picture that shows a bay.

1.    2.

Name: _____

Sequence **WEEK 3 DAY 3**

Read the story. Picture the steps for opening a gift.

Eva, open your gift!
First, pull off the tape.
Next, rip off the paper.
Then, lift off the top to the box.
There is a lot of paper inside.
Pull out that paper.
Finally, dig your hands into the box.
There is the toy you want!

Fill in the circle next to the correct answer.

1. Eva pulls off the tape. Next, she will _____.
   Ⓐ dig inside the box
   Ⓑ rip off the paper
   Ⓒ play with the gift

2. What must Eva do after she rips off the paper?
   Ⓐ pull out the paper
   Ⓑ find the box
   Ⓒ lift off the top to the box

3. What must Eva do to get the gift?
   Ⓐ dig into the box
   Ⓑ pull out the paper
   Ⓒ say thank you

WORD MEANINGS

Circle the word that means about the same as <u>last</u>.

1. first   2. finally   3. next

Name: _____

Sequence **WEEK 3 DAY 4**

Read the story. Remember the order in which Mike does things.

Mike came to Lee's party.
The boys first ran races.
Next, Mike ate three hot dogs.
He had red soda, too.
Then, Mike ate a lot of cake.
Soon after that, he played one
   more game.
Then, Mike got sick.
Lee's dad took Mike home.
Mike went right to bed.

Fill in the circle next to the correct answer.

1. What does Mike do before he eats hot dogs?
   Ⓐ He has some soda.
   Ⓑ He runs races.
   Ⓒ He gets sick.

2. What does Mike do soon after he eats a lot of cake?
   Ⓐ He has red soda.
   Ⓑ He eats one more hot dog.
   Ⓒ He plays one more game.

3. What does Mike do last?
   Ⓐ He goes to a party.
   Ⓑ He eats a lot of food.
   Ⓒ He goes to bed.

WORD MEANINGS

Circle the word that tells <u>when</u>.

1. more   2. soon   3. came   4. too

Name: _____

Sequence **WEEK 3 DAY 5**

Read the story. Remember the things a robin does to build a nest.

A robin works hard to make a nest.
She first gets small sticks.
And she gets weeds.
Then, she puts the weeds with the sticks.
They look like a circle.
Next, the robin adds mud.
The mud makes the nest strong.
Last, a robin finds a lot of grass.
She puts the grass inside the nest.
The grass makes the nest soft.

Fill in the circle next to the correct answer.

1. What does a robin do first to make a nest?
   Ⓐ She gets sticks and weeds.
   Ⓑ She gets mud.
   Ⓒ She gets soft grass.

2. What happens after the circle of weeds and sticks is made?
   Ⓐ Grass is added.
   Ⓑ The robin rests.
   Ⓒ Mud is added.

3. What does a robin do last?
   Ⓐ She sings a song.
   Ⓑ She adds mud to the nest.
   Ⓒ She puts grass inside the nest.

WORD MEANINGS

Circle the one that is <u>soft</u>.

1. a stick　　2. a rock　　3. an apple　　4. a cotton ball

WEEK 4

Compare and Contrast

Students practice Compare and Contrast *by looking at the similarities and differences between two people or things.*

DAY 1

Say: **This week we will practice the reading skill *Compare and Contrast,* or telling how people or things are the same (comparing) and how they are different (contrasting).** Direct students' attention to the illustration, and say that it shows the two main characters in today's story, twins named Dora and Elena. Then read the instructions aloud. Focus students on listening carefully. Say: **Give a thumbs up when you hear how Dora and Elena are the same and a thumbs down when you hear how they are different.** Read the story slowly, pausing after each sentence for the students' responses. After reading, help students complete the first activity by finding the key word in each question. *(alike, different, same)* End with the phonics activity. Ask students to read the story with you, as well as they can, and listen for the words that rhyme with *hair*.

DAY 2

Say: **Some stories tell how two things are the same, or compare, and how they are different, or contrast.** Use the illustration to introduce the two main characters, Tom and Jerry. Read the instructions aloud, and have students follow along while you read the story. Read the story again, with students reading aloud simple words, such as *dog, cat, pets, car*. Then ask students to tell how the pets are alike and different. Draw a Venn diagram to show their responses. If you wish, use simple drawings in the diagram, for the dog, cat, bugs, sun, car, and so on, rather than words. Use the Venn diagram as you complete the first activity. Then do the phonics activity together. Have students first determine the ending sound in *bug* and the letter that spells that sound.

DAY 3

Direct students' attention to the illustration. Say: **Today we will read about how the sun and the moon are alike and how they are different, or how they compare and contrast.** Ask students to suggest words they would expect to read in a story about the sun and moon, such as *sky* and *hot*. Find applicable words in the story. Then read the instructions aloud. Read the story one sentence at a time, with students following along and repeating the sentence as they point to each word. After reading, complete a Venn diagram to show the facts read. Then complete the first activity together, making students aware of the key words *(alike* and *different)* in each item. Complete the phonics activity together.

DAY 4

Tell students that today's story is about a mom and dad who both have jobs. Read the instructions aloud. Then read the story aloud while students follow along. Stop after the first three sentences and ask what is the same about the mom and dad. Read the next three sentences. Ask for facts about the dad's job and list them on the board. Complete the story, and ask for facts about the mom's job, listing them. Read a fact and ask students to call out *Mom* or *Dad* to identify who the fact describes. Then complete the page together. In the first activity, guide students in finding the key words in each item.

DAY 5

Remind students of the reading skill. Then introduce the story and read the instructions aloud. Read the first four sentences, allowing students to read the words they know. Ask students if those sentences tell how birds and bats are alike or different. (alike) Ask students what they think the next part of the story will tell. (how birds and bats are different) Complete the story. Invite students to help make a Venn diagram that shows the facts they read. Incorporate simple drawings as much as possible. Follow the usual procedure for completing the first activity. Have students do the phonics activity with a partner.

Name: _____

Compare and Contrast

WEEK 4 DAY 1

Read the story. Find out how two sisters are alike and different.

Dora and Elena are twins.
They are in the first grade.
They both have brown eyes.
They both have dark hair.
But their hair is not the same.
Dora has long hair.
She likes to wear bows.
Elena's hair is short.
She wears hats more than bows.

Fill in the circle next to the correct answer.

1. How are Dora and Elena alike?
   - Ⓐ They have short hair.
   - Ⓑ They have brown eyes.
   - Ⓒ They like to wear hats.

2. How are Dora and Elena different?
   - Ⓐ Dora is in first grade, but Elena is not.
   - Ⓑ Dora has long hair, but Elena does not.
   - Ⓒ Dora has dark hair, but Elena does not.

3. What is the same about Dora and Elena?
   - Ⓐ They both have short hair.
   - Ⓑ They both are in first grade.
   - Ⓒ They both wear hats.

RHYMING WORDS

Look back at the story.
Circle a word that rhymes with <u>hair</u>.

Name: _____

Compare and Contrast WEEK 4 DAY 2

Read the story. Find ways that two pets are the same and different.

Tom and Jerry are pets.
They both live in the same house.
Tom is a big yellow dog.
He plays tug with a toy.
Jerry is a little black cat.
He likes to get bugs.
But Tom does not.
Tom goes for rides in the car.
But Jerry stays home.
They both like to rest in the sun.

Fill in the circle next to the correct answer.

1. What is the same about Tom and Jerry?
   Ⓐ They both ride in the car.
   Ⓑ They both are yellow.
   Ⓒ They both are pets.

2. How is Tom like Jerry?
   Ⓐ Both pets rest in the sun.
   Ⓑ Tom is black.
   Ⓒ Tom likes bugs.

3. How are Tom and Jerry different?
   Ⓐ Jerry rides in the car, but Tom does not.
   Ⓑ Jerry is a pet, but Tom is not.
   Ⓒ Jerry likes bugs, but Tom does not.

ENDING SOUNDS

Look back at the story.
Circle three words that end with the same sound as <u>bug</u>.

Name: _____

Compare and Contrast — WEEK 4 DAY 3

Read the story. Find out how the sun and moon are alike and different.

The sun and the moon are in the sky.
They both are far, far away.
But they are not the same.
The moon is mostly rock.
It does not make light like
   the sun does.
People have walked on the moon.
The sun is a very hot star.
You can feel the heat it makes.
People cannot go to the sun.
They would melt.

Fill in the circle next to the correct answer.

1. How are the sun and the moon alike?
   Ⓐ They are stars.
   Ⓑ They are very far away.
   Ⓒ They make light.

2. How is the moon different from the sun?
   Ⓐ The moon is a hot star, but the sun is not.
   Ⓑ The moon is close by, but the sun is not.
   Ⓒ The moon is mostly rock, but the sun is not.

3. How is the sun different from the moon?
   Ⓐ The sun makes light, but the moon does not.
   Ⓑ People have gone to the sun, but not to the moon.
   Ⓒ The sun is in the sky, but the moon is not.

VOWEL SOUNDS

Circle the word that has the same vowel sound you hear in <u>light</u>.

1. it   2. sky   3. twin   4. pig

Name: _____

Compare and Contrast

WEEK 4 DAY 4

Read the story. Remember facts about the jobs a mom and dad do.

Mom and Dad both have jobs.
They work during the day.
Their jobs are not the same.
Dad makes toys out of wood.
He has a big room in our home.
That room is his workshop.
Mom has to drive to work.
She works at a store.
She sells books.

Fill in the circle next to the correct answer.

1. What is the same about Mom and Dad?
   Ⓐ They both work at a store.
   Ⓑ They both work at home.
   Ⓒ They both work during the day.

2. How is Mom's job different from Dad's job?
   Ⓐ Mom works at home, but Dad does not.
   Ⓑ Mom drives to her job, but Dad does not.
   Ⓒ Mom works at night, but Dad does not.

3. How is Dad's job different from Mom's?
   Ⓐ Dad works at a store, but Mom does not.
   Ⓑ Dad drives to a workshop, but Mom does not.
   Ⓒ Dad works at home, but Mom does not.

VOWEL SOUNDS

Circle the word that has the same o sound as job.

1. toy   2. home   3. shop   4. room

Name: _____

Compare and Contrast WEEK 4 DAY 5

Read the story. Look for ways that bats and birds are alike and different.

Bats and birds have wings.
They fly in the sky.
Bats like to eat bugs.
Birds eat bugs, too.
But bats and birds are not the same.
Bats have fur.
They have mouths with teeth.
Birds have feathers.
They use beaks for eating.
A baby bat grows inside its mother.
A baby bird grows in an egg.

Fill in the circle next to the correct answer.

1. How is a bat different from a bird?
   Ⓐ A bat has fur, but a bird does not.
   Ⓑ A bat can fly, but a bird cannot.
   Ⓒ A bat eats bugs, but a bird does not.

2. How are birds and bats alike?
   Ⓐ They fly.
   Ⓑ They have fur.
   Ⓒ They have teeth.

3. How is a bird different from a bat?
   Ⓐ A bird has wings, but a bat does not.
   Ⓑ A bird can fly, but a bat cannot.
   Ⓒ A bird has a beak, but a bat does not.

VOWEL SOUNDS

Circle the word that has the same e sound as teeth.

1. egg    2. beak    3. bed

WEEK 5

Fantasy and Reality

Students determine whether a story or specific information within it are fantastic or realistic.

DAY 1

Say: **This week we are going to practice telling the difference between what is make-believe and what can really happen.** Give an example of a familiar story that has both elements. Then direct students' attention to the illustration, and identify the main characters as Ari and his dog Clover. Read the instructions at the top of the page aloud to focus students on listening for what can and cannot happen. Say: **Give a thumbs up when I read something that can happen.** Read the story aloud, pausing for students' responses. Then ask students to share what in the story was make-believe. Invite them to make up a few more fantastical elements about Clover. Then guide students in circling the key words in the items in the first activity. *(make-believe, really do, true)* Complete the sight words activity together.

DAY 2

Direct students' attention to the illustration. Identify the animal as a mole, and ask students what they can tell about moles based on the picture. (dig holes, live in the ground, have long claws, etc.) Then read the instructions aloud. Ask students what they are going to look for as they read. (what is real and what is make-believe) Instruct students to follow along as you read aloud. After reading, repeat some story details. Say: **Nod your head and say *yes* when I say something that is real. Shake your head and say *no* when I say something that can't happen.** Then complete the activities together.

DAY 3

Ask students to share things they know about toy wagons. Then direct students' attention to the illustration. Explain that the main character is José who has a wagon that looks real but does make-believe things. Read the instructions at the top of the page aloud, and ask students to close their eyes while you read. After reading, ask students to share the parts of the story they enjoyed picturing. Read the story again as students follow along. Then ask volunteers to tell a detail from the story. The rest of the class gives a thumbs up if the detail can happen and a thumbs down if it cannot. Lead students in completing the first activity. Have them work with partners to complete the sight words activity.

DAY 4

Remind students that some stories tell things that are make-believe and things that are real. Say: **We will read about a zebra named Zelda who is celebrating her birthday.** Focus students by reading the instructions aloud. Then read one story sentence at a time, with students pointing to each word as they repeat the sentence. After reading, ask what could not be real in the story. Then invite students to make up additional unreal events for Zelda. Guide students in completing the page.

DAY 5

Build background by telling students that a plant needs water and light to grow. Ask how an indoor plant can be given those things. (people provide) Then say: **Let's read about a girl named Bella who has a plant. As we read, ask yourself what is real and what is make-believe. Raise your hand every time you hear something that is make-believe.** Read the story aloud and then talk with students about the real and make-believe elements. Guide students in completing the page.

Name: _____

Fantasy and Reality WEEK 5 DAY 1

Read the story. As you read, notice the things that can and cannot happen.

Ari was going fishing.
He found his fishing pole.
Then he picked up his box.
Clover watched Ari.
She wagged her tail fast.
Clover was Ari's dog.
She liked to go fishing with Ari.
"Let's go, Clover!" said Ari.
Clover put on her hat.
"I'm ready!" Clover said.

Fill in the circle next to the correct answer.

1. What in the story is make-believe?
   Ⓐ A boy talks to a dog.
   Ⓑ A boy has a pet dog.
   Ⓒ A dog puts on a hat.

2. What can a dog really do?
   Ⓐ A dog can watch a boy.
   Ⓑ A dog can put on a hat.
   Ⓒ A dog can talk like a person.

3. Which one is true about Ari?
   Ⓐ Ari likes to fish.
   Ⓑ Ari has a pet cat.
   Ⓒ Ari can wag his tail.

SIGHT WORDS

Circle the word that correctly completes the sentence.

"I have my fishing pole," (liked   said) Ari.

Fantasy and Reality

WEEK 5 DAY 2

Read the story. Ask yourself, "What is real and what is make-believe?"

The mole dug into the dirt.
He used his front paws.
The paws had sharp claws.
The claws dug fast.
Soon the mole had a deep hole.
Then he went to the store.
He got some chairs.
He got a lamp, too.
The mole put the things into the hole.
Then he called his friends.
"Come and see my home," said the mole.

Fill in the circle next to the correct answer.

1. What in the story is real?
   Ⓐ The mole has sharp claws.
   Ⓑ The mole talks like a person.
   Ⓒ The mole goes to a store.

2. What in the story is make-believe?
   Ⓐ A mole digs a hole.
   Ⓑ A mole has paws.
   Ⓒ A mole gets chairs.

3. What can really happen?
   Ⓐ An animal can shop at a store.
   Ⓑ An animal can make a hole in the ground.
   Ⓒ An animal can need a lamp.

SIGHT WORDS

Circle the word that correctly completes the sentence.

The bell will ring (soon   some), and we will go home.

Name: _____

Fantasy and Reality

WEEK 5 DAY 3

Read the story. Picture in your mind what José did.

José got into his red wagon.
He was ready for a ride.
He had an apple in his pocket.
He had a map on his lap.
Best of all, José had his rock.
José asked where he should go.
Then he rubbed the rock.
The answer showed up on it.
So José pulled the wagon's handle.
Two wings came out.
The wagon flew into the air.

Fill in the circle next to the correct answer.

1. What in the story can happen?
   Ⓐ A wagon can have wings.
   Ⓑ A rock can answer a question.
   Ⓒ A boy can have a wagon.

2. What in the story is make-believe?
   Ⓐ A boy has an apple.
   Ⓑ A boy sits in a wagon.
   Ⓒ A boy has a flying wagon.

3. What is magic in the story?
   Ⓐ José and the apple
   Ⓑ the rock and the wagon
   Ⓒ the map and the apple

SIGHT WORDS

Circle the two words that are the same.

1. red   2. read   3. ride   4. ride   5. rode

Fantasy and Reality

WEEK 5 DAY 4

Read the story. Watch for things that cannot be real.

A zebra is like a horse.
But a zebra has stripes.
The stripes are all over its body.
Stripes go down a zebra's legs.
Stripes cover its tail.

A birthday is a special day for a zebra.
On that day, the zebra gets to make a wish.
Today is Zelda Zebra's birthday.
Zelda says, "I want red polka dots, please.
They will look pretty with my black stripes!"

Fill in the circle next to the correct answer.

1. What in the story is real?
   - Ⓐ A zebra has stripes all over its body.
   - Ⓑ A zebra can make a wish on its birthday.
   - Ⓒ A zebra can talk like a person.

2. What in the story is make-believe?
   - Ⓐ A zebra is like a horse.
   - Ⓑ A zebra has stripes on its legs.
   - Ⓒ A zebra wants red polka dots on its body.

3. What can be true about Zelda Zebra?
   - Ⓐ She can have black stripes.
   - Ⓑ She can make a wish.
   - Ⓒ She can know when it is her birthday.

SIGHT WORDS

Write the letters on the lines to spell the word <u>please</u>.

1. ___ ___ease   2. plea___ ___   3. pl___ ___se

Name: _____

Fantasy and Reality — WEEK 5 DAY 5

Read the story. Ask yourself, "What is real and what is make-believe?"

Bella cares for her plant.
She knows what plants need.
Plants need light.
Bella has a lamp in her room.
She lets her plant turn on the lamp.
The plant turns on the light every day.
Plants also need water.
Bella waters her plant every week.
She says, "Open up."
The plant opens its mouth.
Bella sticks in a straw.
She gives the plant a drink.

Fill in the circle next to the correct answer.

1. What in the story is make-believe?
   Ⓐ A plant can sip from a straw.
   Ⓑ A plant can be in a room.
   Ⓒ A plant can need water.

2. What in the story can really happen?
   Ⓐ A girl can care for a plant.
   Ⓑ A plant can turn on a lamp.
   Ⓒ A plant can do as a girl says.

3. Which one is true about plants?
   Ⓐ Plants need a straw.
   Ⓑ Plants need a mouth.
   Ⓒ Plants need water and light.

SIGHT WORDS

Circle the two words that are the same.

1. here   2. her   3. him   4. his   5. her

© Evan-Moor Corp. • EMC 3451 • Daily Reading Comprehension

WEEK 6

Prediction

With Prediction, students use clues from a story and prior knowledge to predict what will happen next. Students understand that good predictions follow logically from the events of the story.

DAY 1

Tell students that this week they will be practicing a reading skill called *Prediction*. Say: **To predict means to make a good guess about what may happen next. Good readers pay attention to what a character says and does. They use those clues to predict what will probably happen.** Direct students' attention to the story and the illustration of a little boy named Zack. Read the instructions at the top of the page aloud. Then read the story aloud, inviting students to follow along and read the words they know. After reading, guide students in completing the first activity. Let students tell the story clues that help them answer the items. Complete the word meanings activity together.

DAY 2

Remind students of the reading skill by recalling the prediction made about Zack in the story for Day 1. (Zack will probably put his shoes on wrong.) Ask students to recall the clues that helped them make the prediction. (Zack put on all of his clothes wrong.) Then direct students' attention to the illustration on page 42. Say: **Today we will read a story about what happens when a hen lays eggs.** Read the instructions aloud, and remind students to look for clues that will help them make a prediction. Ask students to follow along as you read aloud. After reading, help them complete the first activity. Let them defend their answer choices, guiding them to use clues from the story. Complete the word meanings activity together, letting students make the animal sounds that are the answers.

DAY 3

Tell students that today they will make a prediction after reading a story about a boy named Ty and his sister Nell. Remind them to pay close attention to story clues—what the characters say and do. Read the instructions aloud. Then read the story aloud, asking students to follow along and read the words they know. After reading, guide students in completing the first activity. Refer them to story clues to help choose their responses. Then complete the word meanings activity together. Say: **Stories often have clues about what words mean.** Refer to the parts of the story that tell about Nell grabbing things.

DAY 4

Direct students' attention to the illustration. Say: **Today's story tells how a spider gets its food.** Have students identify the web in the picture. Then read the instructions aloud. Invite students to follow as you read aloud and to read the words they know, if only *spider* and *web*. After reading, complete the first activity together. Let students explain the story clues that help them make predictions. Instruct students to do the word meanings activity independently, and then call on individuals to share their answers.

DAY 5

Invite students to tell a partner what they know about making predictions while reading. Allow sharing of responses. Then read the instructions aloud. Read the story aloud as students follow along. Refer to story clues to complete the first activity. Then guide students to refer back to the story for words that tell what Lily did with the balls of snow. (rolled, patted) Read the instructions for the word meanings activity, and have students circle the picture that shows Lily patting the ball of snow.

Name: _____

Prediction WEEK 6 DAY 1

Read the story. Ask yourself, "What will probably happen next?"

Zack is three years old.
He is getting dressed.
He wants to dress by himself.
So Zack puts on his pants.
The zipper is in the back.
He puts on his shirt.
The tag is on the outside.
He pulls on his socks.
One sock is white.
The other sock is red.
Then Zack gets his shoes.

Fill in the circle next to the correct answer.

1. What is wrong with Zack's socks?
   Ⓐ The socks are on his hands.
   Ⓑ The socks are too small.
   Ⓒ The socks are different colors.

2. What will Zack probably do next?
   Ⓐ put on his shoes the right way
   Ⓑ tie his shoes the right way
   Ⓒ put on his shoes the wrong way

3. Why do you think that Zack will have trouble putting on his shoes?
   Ⓐ Zack's shoes are too small.
   Ⓑ Zack put his clothes on wrong.
   Ⓒ Zack does not like wearing shoes.

WORD MEANINGS

Circle what the word <u>dress</u> means in this sentence:

Zack wants to dress by himself.

1.    2.

Name: _____

WEEK 6
Prediction **DAY 2**

Read the story. Ask yourself, "What will probably happen next?"

The hen sat on the eggs.
Her feathers were fluffy.
They kept the eggs warm.
Each day, the hen turned the eggs.
She turned them with her beak.
She warmed every part of the eggs.
One day the eggs started to crack.
The chicks peeped inside the eggs.
The hen clucked.
She told the chicks to come out.

Fill in the circle next to the correct answer.

1. What will probably happen next?
   Ⓐ The chicks will break out of their eggs.
   Ⓑ The hen will sit on the eggs.
   Ⓒ The chicks will lay eggs.

2. Where does a chick grow?
   Ⓐ inside an egg
   Ⓑ inside a hen
   Ⓒ in the water

3. What will probably happen the next time the hen lays eggs?
   Ⓐ She will keep the eggs warm.
   Ⓑ She will crack the eggs with her beak.
   Ⓒ She will color the eggs.

WORD MEANINGS

Circle the sound each animal makes.

1. hen   (quack   cluck)
2. chick   (cluck   peep)

42   Daily Reading Comprehension • EMC 3451 • © Evan-Moor Corp.

Name: _____

Prediction — **WEEK 6 DAY 3**

Read the story. Ask yourself, "What will probably happen next?"

Ty's mom is shopping for food.
Ty pushes his sister Nell in the cart.
Nell likes to grab things.
She wants to get a can of peas.
"Don't touch," says Ty.
Nell takes an apple.
"Put that back," says Ty.
Nell tries to get a shiny pan.
Ty says, "No no no!"
Then Ty stops to tie his shoe.

Fill in the circle next to the correct answer.

1. What will probably happen next?
   - Ⓐ Nell will try to grab something.
   - Ⓑ Ty will hug his sister.
   - Ⓒ Nell will go to sleep.

2. Which one tells about Nell?
   - Ⓐ Nell is older than Ty.
   - Ⓑ Nell listens to Ty.
   - Ⓒ Nell does not listen to Ty.

3. What might happen if Ty did not stop to tie his shoe?
   - Ⓐ He could not push the cart.
   - Ⓑ His mom would be mad.
   - Ⓒ He could trip and fall.

WORD MEANINGS

Circle what it means to grab.

1. to get   2. to tell   3. to give

© Evan-Moor Corp. • EMC 3451 • Daily Reading Comprehension

Name: _____

Prediction — WEEK 6 DAY 4

Read the story. Ask yourself, "What will probably happen next?"

The spider wants food.
She likes to eat bugs.
So she makes a trap.
The spider spins a sticky web.
Round and round she goes.
Up and down she goes.
Then she waits.
The web is hard for bugs to see.
Whap! A bug flies into the web.
The web shakes when the bug lands.
The bug is stuck.

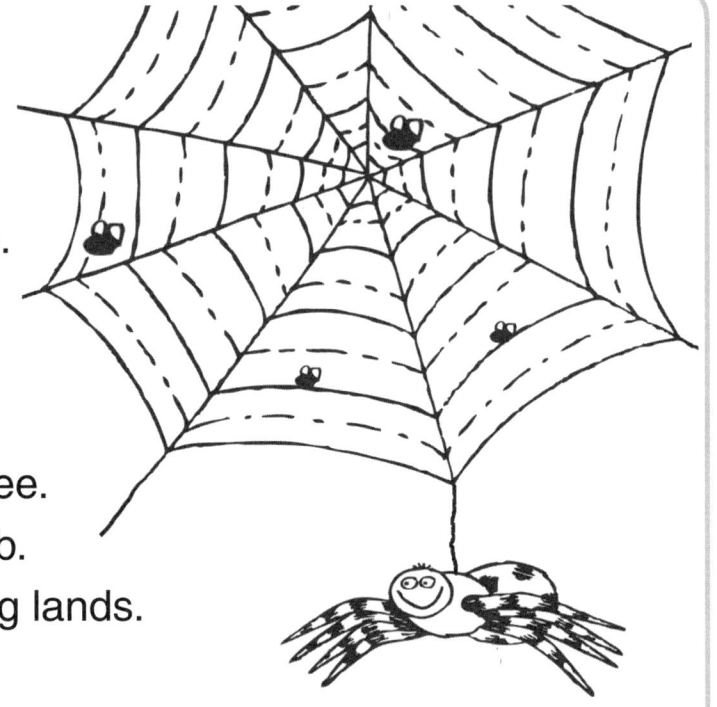

Fill in the circle next to the correct answer.

1. What will probably happen next?
   Ⓐ The spider will let the bug go.
   Ⓑ The bug will fly away.
   Ⓒ The spider will eat the bug.

2. Why does a spider spin a web?
   Ⓐ to make a home
   Ⓑ to trap bugs
   Ⓒ to play with bugs

3. What will a spider probably do if a big storm blows down her web?
   Ⓐ She will spin a new web.
   Ⓑ She will go to sleep.
   Ⓒ She will eat plants.

WORD MEANINGS

Look around the classroom.
On the line, write the name of something you see that is <u>sticky</u>.

_____

Name: _____

Prediction WEEK 6 DAY 5

Read the story. Ask yourself, "What will probably happen next?"

Lily made a little snowball.
Then she rolled the ball in the snow.
She rolled it over and over.
The ball got bigger and bigger.
Lily patted the big ball.
She made a second ball in the same way.
That ball was smaller than the first.
Lily rolled one more ball.
That ball was the smallest.
Now she was ready to stack the balls.

Fill in the circle next to the correct answer.

1. What will Lily probably do next?
   Ⓐ Lily will throw the balls of snow.
   Ⓑ Lily will play in the park.
   Ⓒ Lily will make a snowman.

2. What happens when Lily rolls the snowball?
   Ⓐ The snowball gets bigger.
   Ⓑ The snowball gets smaller.
   Ⓒ The snowball gets colder.

3. What will Lily probably do with the smallest snowball?
   Ⓐ put it under the biggest snowball
   Ⓑ put it on top of the other two snowballs
   Ⓒ put it between the other two snowballs

WORD MEANINGS

Circle the picture that shows how Lily <u>patted</u> the ball of snow.

1.    2.

© Evan-Moor Corp. • EMC 3451 • Daily Reading Comprehension

WEEK 7

Main Idea
Students read to understand the central message of a passage or story.

DAY 1
Tell students that this week they will practice the reading skill *Main Idea*. Recall that the main idea is what a story is mostly about. Direct students' attention to the illustration. Say: **Pictures often give clues about the main idea. What do you think this story is about?** Then read the instructions aloud. Ask students to follow along as you read the story. After reading, evaluate whether students' guesses about the main idea were correct. Complete the first activity together. Take time helping students answer each item and understanding why two choices are incorrect. Have students complete the phonics activity with a partner. Go over their answers together.

DAY 2
Begin by asking students to recall the main idea of yesterday's story. (Pig bakes the best pies in town.) Then direct students' attention to the illustration of today's story, and ask students to guess the main character. (a small owl) Explain that the main idea will have something to do with the owl. Point to the cactus in the illustration. Let students find *cactus* in the story and read the word out loud. Then read the instructions aloud, and ask students to follow along as you read. After reading, ask: **Is the story about the owl?** (yes) Guide students in completing the first activity and in understanding why some choices are incorrect. Do the phonics activity together. Help students first determine the beginning sound in *top* and the letter that spells that sound. Tell students to look in the story for two other words that begin with /t/. (e.g., *tiny, tall*)

DAY 3
Review the skill. Then direct students' attention to the illustration. Tell them that it shows the main character, a girl named Tamika. Ask: **Will the main idea have something to do with Tamika?** (yes) Read the instructions aloud. Then read one sentence of the story at a time, and pause for students to read and repeat the sentence. After reading, lead students in completing the first activity and in understanding the correct answers. Do the phonics activity together, with students giving a thumbs up when they hear the same ending sound as in *funny*.

DAY 4
Direct students' attention to the illustration, and elicit ideas for what the story is about. Remind students that what a story is mostly about is called the *Main Idea*. Read the instructions aloud. After reading the story, help students complete the activities.

DAY 5
Remind students of the skill. Then direct students' attention to the illustration. Ask: **What animal is the main character in this story?** (a hippo) **What animal will the main idea be about?** (a hippo) Read the instructions aloud. Tell students that they should also listen carefully for facts about the hippo. After reading the story, ask students what they remember about hippos. Then guide students in completing the activities on the page.

Name: _____

WEEK 7
Main Idea   DAY 1

Read the story. Ask yourself, "What is this story about?"

Pig bakes the best pies in town.
Her pies win prizes.
Pig sells the pies at her pie shop.
She makes pies with fruit.
And she makes pies with whipped cream.
All of her pies are big.
Little Bear loves eating Pig's pies.
He keeps eating more and more.
Little Bear is sure to be Big Bear soon!

Fill in the circle next to the correct answer.

1. What is the story about?
   Ⓐ Little Bear eats too many pies.
   Ⓑ Pig bakes the best pies in town.
   Ⓒ Pig makes big pies.

2. Which one tells about Pig?
   Ⓐ Pig only makes fruit pies.
   Ⓑ Pig makes small pies.
   Ⓒ Pig has a pie shop.

3. Which one tells about Little Bear?
   Ⓐ Little Bear is a big bear.
   Ⓑ Little Bear likes to eat pies.
   Ⓒ Little Bear wins prizes.

BEGINNING SOUNDS

Circle the pairs of words that begin with the same sounds.

1. Big Bear   2. Pig's Pies   3. Big Pig

Name: _____

Main Idea **WEEK 7 DAY 2**

Read the story. Ask yourself, "What is this story about?"

A tiny owl is looking for a home.
She can live where it is hot.
The owl flies to a cactus plant.
The cactus is as tall as a tree.
A hole is near the top.
The owl goes in.
The hole is just the right size.
The tiny owl can live inside this hole.
She can lay eggs inside, too.
The cactus will be a good home
   for the tiny owl.

Fill in the circle next to the correct answer.

1. What is the story about?
   Ⓐ An owl lays eggs.
   Ⓑ An owl looks for a place to live.
   Ⓒ A cactus plant has a hole.

2. Which one tells about the cactus?
   Ⓐ The cactus is small like a flower.
   Ⓑ The cactus has eggs inside.
   Ⓒ The cactus has a hole in it.

3. Which one tells about the owl?
   Ⓐ The owl is very big.
   Ⓑ The owl lives in a tree.
   Ⓒ The owl is very small.

BEGINNING SOUNDS

Look back at the story.
Circle two words that start with the same sound you hear in <u>top</u>.

Name: _____

WEEK 7
Main Idea **DAY 3**

Read the story. Ask yourself, "What is this story about?"

The day was cold.
The day was icy.
"What a great day!" said Tamika.
She dressed in her warm clothes.
Then she and her dad ran to the pond.
The ice made the pond shine.
Tamika laced her skates.
Dad made sure that the ice was thick.
Then Tamika skated round and round.

Fill in the circle next to the correct answer.

1. The story is about _____.
   Ⓐ a very cold day
   Ⓑ an icy pond
   Ⓒ a girl skating on a pond

2. What is good about the cold and icy day?
   Ⓐ Tamika can play in the snow.
   Ⓑ Tamika can skate on the pond.
   Ⓒ Tamika can wear her warm clothes.

3. Which one tells about the pond in the story?
   Ⓐ The pond has thick ice.
   Ⓑ The pond is good for fishing.
   Ⓒ The pond is good for washing.

VOWEL SOUNDS

Circle the word that ends with the same sound you hear in <u>funny</u>.

1. day   2. fly   3. icy   4. they

© Evan-Moor Corp. • EMC 3451 • Daily Reading Comprehension

Name: _____

WEEK 7
Main Idea **DAY 4**

Read the story. Ask yourself, "What is this story about?"

Alex and Nate were bored.
Nate wanted to play with toy cars.
But Alex wanted to play a new game.
"I know! Let's play car wash!" said Alex.
The boys put their toy cars in a line.
Nate covered the cars with soap.
Alex washed off the soap with a hose.
The cars and the boys got very wet.
The car wash was a boy wash, too!

Fill in the circle next to the correct answer.

1. What is the story about?
   Ⓐ Two boys are bored.
   Ⓑ Two boys play with toy cars.
   Ⓒ Two boys take a bath.

2. What does the last sentence in the story mean?
   Ⓐ The boys got wet and soapy.
   Ⓑ Nate put soap on Alex.
   Ⓒ Alex wet Nate with the hose.

3. Which one tells about Alex?
   Ⓐ Alex wants more toy cars.
   Ⓑ Alex likes to play the same thing over and over.
   Ⓒ Alex likes to play new games.

BEGINNING SOUNDS

Look back at the story.
Circle two words that begin with the same sound you hear in <u>want</u>.

Name: _____

Main Idea — WEEK 7, DAY 5

Read the story. Ask yourself, "What is this story about?"

The sun can burn a hippo.
So a hippo stays in water.
The water keeps a hippo cool.
It will stay in water for most of the day.
A hippo can go deep into the water.
Just the top of its head sticks out.
A hippo comes out of the water to eat.
It eats at night.
It eats after the hot sun goes down.

Fill in the circle next to the correct answer.

1. What is the story about?
   Ⓐ A hippo eats at night.
   Ⓑ A hippo stays out of the sun.
   Ⓒ A hippo is very big.

2. What is true about a hippo?
   Ⓐ A hippo can go deep into the water.
   Ⓑ A hippo eats most of the day.
   Ⓒ A hippo likes the hot sun.

3. Which one does a hippo do at night?

   Ⓐ

   Ⓑ

   Ⓒ

ENDING SOUNDS

Read the first sentence in the story.
Circle the three words that have the same ending sound.

WEEK 8

Who and What

Students read to determine "who" (the main character) and "what" (the main character's actions).

DAY 1

Tell students that this week they will practice finding the main character in stories and paying attention to what the character does. Say: **The main character is the person or thing the story is mostly about.** Direct students' attention to the illustration. Say: **This picture gives clues about the main character. What do you think the main character is?** (cat) **Let's read the story to find out the cat's name and what the cat does.** Read the instructions at the top of the page aloud. Then read the story as students follow along. Guide students to complete the first activity. With each item, help students locate the answer in the story and reread those sentences. Have students do the sight words activity with a partner. They should read all the words out loud before deciding on their answers. Check students' answers together.

DAY 2

Review the skill of *Who and What* by asking students to respond *yes* or *no* to the following statements: **(1) The main character in a story can be a person.** (yes) **(2) Animals can be the main characters.** (yes) **(3) Some stories are about people *and* animals.** (yes) Then direct students' attention to the story. Ask them to identify words they can read. Read the instructions aloud, and invite students to read the story along with you. After reading, ask students to tell the main character to a partner. Then lead students in completing the first activity. For items 2 and 3, reread the sentences containing the answers. Complete the sight words activity, following the procedure used on Day 1.

DAY 3

Direct students' attention to the illustration of a teacher and students. Say: **Let's read the story to see if there is one main character or two.** Read the instructions aloud, and then read the story as students follow along. You may choose to reread the story, with some students reading with you and others acting it out. After reading, ask students to show with their fingers the number of main characters. (one) Help students understand that most of the story is about Ben. Then guide them in completing the first activity. For each item, read the sentence(s) in the story that support the correct answer. Instruct students to do the sight words activity with a partner. Go over their answers together.

DAY 4

Review the skill. Then direct students' attention to the illustration. Say: **This picture gives clues about the main character. But the picture does not give enough information. We need to read to find out the kind of bear it is and what that bear is doing.** Read the instructions aloud. Read each story sentence aloud, and have students read it after you, touching each word as they say it. Guide students in completing the activities.

DAY 5

Remind students of the skill. Then say: **Today we're going to read a poem. Poems have main characters, too, just like stories.** Read the instructions aloud, and then read the poem aloud as students follow along. Reread the poem as students read the words they know. Help students do the first activity. For item 1, point out that both words in the answer choice must be correct. Complete the sight words activity together, modeling for students how to read the sentence and insert each answer choice.

Name: _____

Who and What

WEEK 8
DAY 1

Read the story. Think about the main character and what the character does.

Rosa has a cat named Puff.
He likes to play a game.
Rosa throws a toy mouse.
Puff runs after the mouse.
He picks it up in his mouth.
Puff brings the toy back to Rosa.
Rosa throws the toy over and over.
Puff plays for a long time.
Then he takes a nap.
Puff needs to rest.
Then he can play again!

Fill in the circle next to the correct answer.

1. What is Puff?
   Ⓐ a girl
   Ⓑ a mouse
   Ⓒ a cat

2. What does Rosa like to do?
   Ⓐ Rosa likes to chase a toy mouse.
   Ⓑ Rosa likes to take a nap.
   Ⓒ Rosa likes to play with her cat.

3. Which one does Puff play with?
   Ⓐ
   Ⓑ
   Ⓒ

SIGHT WORDS

Circle the two words that are the same.

1. then   2. them   3. than   4. then   5. they

Name: _____

Who and What WEEK 8 DAY 2

Read the story. Think about bats and what they do.

Bats have wings.
The wings are made of skin.
Bats use their wings to fly.
They fly to catch bugs.
Then they eat them up.
Bats use their wings when they rest, too.
Bats hang upside down from their feet.
They fold their wings around their bodies.
They stay warm and cozy.

Fill in the circle next to the correct answer.

1. What is the story about?
   Ⓐ how bats use their wings
   Ⓑ why bats hang upside down
   Ⓒ what kinds of bugs bats eat

2. Bats use their wings to _____.
   Ⓐ wave at bugs
   Ⓑ stay warm
   Ⓒ swim in water

3. A bat's wings are made of _____.
   Ⓐ skin
   Ⓑ hair
   Ⓒ clay

SIGHT WORDS

Circle the two words that are the same.

1. use   2. up   3. under   4. use   5. us

Name: _____

Who and What — WEEK 8, DAY 3

Read the story. Ask yourself, "What is the main character doing?"

The teacher rings a bell.
Ben knows what that bell means.
It is story time!
Ben knows what to do.
He takes three big steps to the rug.
He plops down, and he crosses his legs.
Then he places his hands in his lap.
Ben smiles at his teacher.
He is ready for a story.
Ben thinks story time is the best time!

Fill in the circle next to the correct answer.

1. Who rings a bell?
   - Ⓐ Ben
   - Ⓑ a teacher
   - Ⓒ a friend

2. What does the bell mean?
   - Ⓐ It is time to eat.
   - Ⓑ It is time to play.
   - Ⓒ It is time for a story.

3. What is the first thing Ben does when he hears the bell?
   - Ⓐ Ben sits on the rug.
   - Ⓑ Ben smiles at his teacher.
   - Ⓒ Ben walks to the rug.

SIGHT WORDS

Circle the two words that are the same.

1. has   2. his   3. her   4. him   5. his

© Evan-Moor Corp. • EMC 3451 • Daily Reading Comprehension

Name: _____

Who and What

WEEK 8
DAY 4

Read the story. Ask yourself, "What are the main characters doing?"

Some black bears make homes in trees.
They make nests in trees to rest in.
The bears use their claws to climb high.
They find a safe place.
Then the bears break off tree parts.
They put them this way and that.
They build strong nests.
A nest must be strong to hold a bear!

Fill in the circle next to the correct answer.

1. The main characters are _____.
   Ⓐ brown bears
   Ⓑ white bears
   Ⓒ black bears

2. What do some black bears do?
   Ⓐ Some black bears make nests in trees.
   Ⓑ Some black bears make nests on the ground.
   Ⓒ Some black bears make tree parts.

3. What do the bears use to make nests?
   Ⓐ piles of grass
   Ⓑ a lot of leaves
   Ⓒ parts of trees

SIGHT WORDS

Circle the word that correctly completes the sentence.

Emma (play   put) the toy bear on her bed.

Name: _____

Week 8
Who and What
Day 5

Read the poem. Think about the main character and what the character does.

> I have a little hamster.
> He really likes to eat.
> He holds a seed in his paws.
> And he nibbles up the treat.
>
> I have a little hamster.
> He really likes to run.
> He races around a wheel.
> And he climbs to have some fun.

Fill in the circle next to the correct answer.

1. What does the hamster like to do?
   Ⓐ play and rest
   Ⓑ sleep and eat
   Ⓒ play and eat

2. Which one tells about a hamster?
   Ⓐ A hamster mostly sleeps.
   Ⓑ A hamster is a big animal.
   Ⓒ A hamster can be a pet.

3. What is a good toy for a hamster?
   Ⓐ a wheel to run in
   Ⓑ some seeds to throw
   Ⓒ a bone to chew

SIGHT WORDS

Circle the word that correctly completes the sentence.

A hamster likes to (eat   ate) seeds and nuts.

WEEK 9

Sequence

Students practice Sequence to determine the order of events or steps in a process.

DAY 1

Tell students that this week they will practice a reading skill called *Sequence*. Review for students that *Sequence* is the order in which things happen. Say: **Good readers look for signal words that help them understand when things happen. The signal words in today's story are the days of the week.** Review the order of the days of the week. Then help students scan the story and circle the days mentioned. (*Sunday, Monday, Tuesday*) Then read the last sentence and ask what day is *the next day*. (Wednesday) Read the instructions aloud and remind students to use the signal words as helpers. Read the first four sentences of the story aloud. Pause to review with students what the dogs did on that day. Continue in this way until the entire story is read. Then guide students through the first activity. Take time to show them how to think through the answers. Let students do the word meanings activity independently and then hold up one or two fingers to indicate their answers.

DAY 2

Remind students of the skill, and review the importance of signal words. Direct students' attention to the illustration, and identify the boy as Noah. Read the instructions aloud, and explain that signal words will help tell the order in which Noah puts on his clothes. Write the words *First, Next, then, Then,* and *Finally* on the board and read them with students. Instruct students to look for these words as the story is read. Point out that signal words are often, but not always, the first word in a sentence. Read the story aloud as students follow along. Then guide students through the first activity by first circling the signal words. (*first, last, just before*) Read the instructions for the word meanings activity. Say: **Good readers look back to a story for clues about what words mean.** Guide students to find *poked out* in the story and to read the sentence out loud with you. Let students hold up one or two fingers to indicate the answer. (two)

DAY 3

Remind students of the skill. Say: **Sequence is important in following instructions to do something.** Read the instructions and the story aloud as students follow along, looking for signal words that tell the order of the steps in making seed wiggles. Ask them to read out loud the signal words when you come to them. After reading, ask students to show with their fingers the number of steps it takes to make seed wiggles. (six) Lead students in completing the first activity by first circling the signal words in items 1 and 2. (*second, right after*) Complete the word meanings activity together. Ask students to wiggle their fingers and then circle the picture that shows a wiggly line.

DAY 4

Remind students of the skill. Then direct their attention to the illustration, and identify the people as Brad and his family. Say that the story tells what the family does on one day of a trip. Read the story aloud as students follow along. After each sentence, ask students if they noticed any signal words. (*In the morning, in the afternoon, at night*) Guide students in completing the first activity by circling the key words and showing how to use the signal words in the story to find the answers quickly. Complete the word meanings activity together.

DAY 5

Remind students of the skill. Tell them they are going to read about sea turtles. Then read the instructions aloud. Read the first six lines as students follow along. Stop and ask them to circle the signal words. (*first, Next, Then*) Then read the rest of the story, having students circle the signal words. (*Then, At last*) Complete the activities together.

Name: _____

WEEK 9
Sequence DAY 1

Read the story. Ask yourself, "What do the dogs do on each day?"

Wags and Penny played together.
They played hide-and-seek on Sunday.
Penny hid under the bed.
Wags hid behind a plant.
On Monday they dug holes in the yard.
Penny hid a bone.
Wags dug up some flowers.
They played with balls on Tuesday.
Penny chased her ball.
Wags chewed his ball to bits.
The dogs played tug the next day.

Fill in the circle next to the correct answer.

1. What do the dogs do first?
   Ⓐ They play tug.
   Ⓑ They dig holes in the yard.
   Ⓒ They play hide-and-seek.

2. What do the dogs do on Wednesday?
   Ⓐ They play tug.
   Ⓑ They play with balls.
   Ⓒ They rest.

3. What does Wags do before he chews up his ball?
   Ⓐ He hides a bone.
   Ⓑ He digs up some flowers.
   Ⓒ He plays tag.

WORD MEANINGS

Circle the picture that shows a ball chewed to <u>bits</u>.

1.    2.

Name: _____

Sequence — **WEEK 9 DAY 2**

Read the story. Ask yourself, "What are the steps Noah takes to get dressed?"

Noah got ready to play outside.
First, he put on his snow pants.
Next, he put on his jacket.
He then pulled on his long hat.
Then, Noah tugged on his snow boots.
All he needed were his gloves.
Uh-oh!
He found only one glove to put on.
Noah looked in the mirror.
Fingers poked out from under his hat.
There was the missing glove!
Finally, Noah was ready to play.

Fill in the circle next to the correct answer.

1. What does Noah put on first?
   - Ⓐ snow pants
   - Ⓑ gloves
   - Ⓒ a jacket

2. What does Noah put on last?
   - Ⓐ boots
   - Ⓑ mittens
   - Ⓒ gloves

3. What does Noah put on just before his snow boots?
   - Ⓐ a jacket
   - Ⓑ snow pants
   - Ⓒ a long hat

WORD MEANINGS

Circle the rabbit that is <u>poking out</u>.

1.   2.

Name: _____

WEEK 9
Sequence **DAY 3**

Read the directions. Ask yourself, "How do I make seed wiggles?"

Seed wiggles are easy to make.
First, use glue to draw a wiggly line.
Draw the line on waxed paper.
Make the line wide and smooth.
Second, shake seeds onto the line.
Cover every bit of the glue.
Third, let the wiggly line dry overnight.
Fourth, peel the paper off the seed wiggle.
Fifth, make a hole in the seed wiggle.
Sixth, tie string through the hole.
You can hang the wiggle in a window.

Fill in the circle next to the correct answer.

1. What is the second step in making a seed wiggle?
   Ⓐ Draw a wiggly line.
   Ⓑ Peel off the waxed paper.
   Ⓒ Shake seeds onto the line.

2. Which step comes right after the third step?
   Ⓐ the fourth step
   Ⓑ the second step
   Ⓒ the fifth step

3. Which step tells to tie string to the seed wiggle?
   Ⓐ the sixth step
   Ⓑ the third step
   Ⓒ the fifth step

WORD MEANINGS

Circle the wiggly line.

1. ∿∿∿   2. ———   3. ⌒

Name: _____

Sequence — WEEK 9, DAY 4

Read the story. Ask yourself, "What does the family do?"

Brad's family took a trip.
They stayed in a cabin at Pine Lake.
In the morning, they packed some food.
Then they rode a boat on the lake.
They all tried to catch the biggest fish.
They swam in the afternoon.
Then they walked on some trails.
Brad's family played games at night.
They fell asleep to the sound of crickets.

Fill in the circle next to the correct answer.

1. What is the first thing Brad's family does?
   Ⓐ They fish.
   Ⓑ They pack some food.
   Ⓒ They ride in a boat.

2. What does Brad's family do in the afternoon?
   Ⓐ They play games.
   Ⓑ They fall asleep.
   Ⓒ They take a walk.

3. What does the family do right before they fall asleep?
   Ⓐ They play games.
   Ⓑ They walk.
   Ⓒ They eat fish.

WORD MEANINGS

Circle all of the words that tell <u>when</u> things happened.

in the morning   at night   at the lake   in the afternoon

Name: _____

WEEK 9
Sequence **DAY 5**

Read the story. Ask yourself, "How are sea turtles born?"

Sea turtles are born on a beach.
The mother turtle first digs a hole.
She uses her back feet.
Next, she lays her eggs in the hole.
She covers the eggs with sand.
Then, she walks away.
The warm sun helps the eggs hatch.
The baby sea turtles wait until night.
Then, they dig out of the sand.
They crawl across the beach.
At last, they go into the sea.

Fill in the circle next to the correct answer.

1. What is the last thing that a mother sea turtle does?
   Ⓐ She walks away from the eggs.
   Ⓑ She digs a hole in the sand.
   Ⓒ She covers the eggs with sand.

2. What do the babies do right after they hatch?
   Ⓐ They go into the sea.
   Ⓑ They dig out of the sand.
   Ⓒ They wait until it is dark.

3. What do baby sea turtles do after they dig out of the sand?
   Ⓐ They hatch from an egg.
   Ⓑ They crawl across the sand.
   Ⓒ They wait until the sun is out.

WORD MEANINGS

Circle what it means to <u>hatch</u>.

1. to go into an egg   2. to come out of an egg

© Evan-Moor Corp. • EMC 3451 • Daily Reading Comprehension

WEEK 10

Compare and Contrast

Students practice Compare and Contrast *by looking at the similarities and differences between two people or things.*

DAY 1

Say: **This week we will practice the reading skill of *Compare and Contrast*, or telling how people or things are the same (comparing) and how they are different (contrasting).** Direct attention to the illustration, and identify the two main characters as Leroy and Will. Read the instructions aloud. Then read the first two sentences. Ask students if those sentences tell how Leroy and Will are alike or different. (alike) Help students discover the signal words that tell the boys are being compared. *(same, both)* Read the rest of the story. Ask if the sentences tell what is the same or what is different between the boys. *(different)* Write *Leroy* and *Will* on the board. Have students contrast, in pictures or words, the ways the boys get to school and the homes they live in. Guide students in completing the first activity by having them first find and circle the signal words. *(same, different, different)* Have students do the phonics activity in pairs. Check the answers together.

DAY 2

Draw a two-part Venn diagram on the board. Label the sections *apples, both, oranges.* Review the reading skill. Then read the instructions aloud. Read the first sentence and ask students if it tells how the fruit are the same or different. (same) Ask students to name the signal word in the sentence. *(both)* Write *are fruits* in the *both* section of the diagram. Say: **As I read the rest of the story, look for facts to complete the diagram.** Read the story slowly, and then guide students to complete the Venn diagram. *(apples—black seeds, can eat skin, doesn't have parts; oranges—white seeds, don't eat skin, has parts; both—are fruits, have seeds inside, have skin, are good for you)* Complete the activities together.

DAY 3

Remind students of the skill. Direct students' attention to the illustration, and identify the characters as Joey and his mom and dad. Read the instructions aloud. Then read aloud the first two sentences and ask students to call out the signal word. *(both)* Ask: **What is the same about Joey's mom and dad?** (They both get him ready for bed.) **What do you expect the next sentences to tell?** (how they are different in getting Joey ready) Read the rest of the story together. Let boys read the sentences about Joey's dad and girls read the sentences about Joey's mom. Then guide students in completing the first activity. For the phonics activity, ask students to give a thumbs up when they hear the long *i* sound and a thumbs down when they don't.

DAY 4

Tell students that they will read about a brother and sister named Abe and Stella. Then read the instructions aloud. Read the story as students follow along, reading the words they know. Use a Venn diagram to compare and contrast the children. Help students complete the first activity by first circling the key word in the item. *(same, different, different)* Students may use the Venn diagram while answering the items. Then guide students through the phonics activity. Let them find words ending in *s*. Then help them differentiate when the *s* stands for the *s* sound and when the *s* stands for the *z* sound.

DAY 5

Remind students of the skill. Then direct their attention to the illustration, and have students identify the animals. Read the instructions aloud. Then read the story and help students notice when the birds are compared and when they are contrasted. Use the customary procedure to complete the first activity. Use the Day 4 procedure for completing the phonics activity.

Name: _____

Compare and Contrast — WEEK 10 DAY 1

Read the story. Ask, "How are the boys the same and how are they different?"

Leroy and Will go to the same school.
They are both in first grade.
Leroy rides a bus to school.
He lives far away.
Will has never been on a bus.
His mom drives him to school.
Will lives in a tall building in the city.
The cars below look small from his window.
Leroy lives in a house.
He can see a sky full of stars from his porch.

Fill in the circle next to the correct answer.

1. What is the same about Leroy and Will?
   - Ⓐ They ride the same school bus.
   - Ⓑ They live next door to each other.
   - Ⓒ They are in the same school.

2. How is Leroy different from Will?
   - Ⓐ Leroy is in first grade, but Will is not.
   - Ⓑ Leroy lives in the city, but Will does not.
   - Ⓒ Leroy rides a bus to school, but Will does not.

3. How are Will and Leroy different?
   - Ⓐ Will's mom drives him to school, but Leroy's mom does not.
   - Ⓑ Leroy lives in a tall building, but Will does not.
   - Ⓒ Will is in second grade, but Leroy is not.

BEGINNING SOUNDS

Read each word. Circle the sound of the letter c.

1. city   s   k
2. car   s   k

Name: _____

Compare and Contrast

WEEK 10 DAY 2

Read the story. Find out how apples and oranges are the same and different.

Apples and oranges are both fruit.
They grow on trees.
And they both have seeds on the inside.
Oranges have white seeds.
Apple seeds are black.
An apple and an orange both have skin.
You have to peel off the skin of an orange.
You can eat an apple's skin.
An orange has parts inside, but an apple does not.
Both fruits are good for you.

Fill in the circle next to the correct answer.

1. How are apples and oranges the same?
   Ⓐ They both come in parts.
   Ⓑ They both grow on trees.
   Ⓒ They both have black seeds.

2. How is an orange different from an apple?
   Ⓐ An orange has parts, but an apple does not.
   Ⓑ An orange is good for you, but an apple is not.
   Ⓒ An orange is a fruit, but an apple is not.

3. Both apple seeds and orange seeds _____.
   Ⓐ are black
   Ⓑ are inside the fruit
   Ⓒ have skin

VOWEL SOUNDS

Circle the words that have the same vowel sound you hear in <u>she</u>.

1. peel   2. tree   3. eat   4. went   5. hen   6. seed

Name: _____

Compare and Contrast — WEEK 10, DAY 3

Read the story. Look for ways the parents are the same and different.

It is time for Joey to go to bed.
Joey's mom and dad both get him ready.
His mom helps Joey put away his toys.
His dad makes sure Joey washes up.
He checks that Joey brushes his teeth.
Joey's mom helps him button his pajamas.
She reads Joey a story when he is in bed.
His dad fluffs Joey's pillow.
They both kiss Joey good night.

Fill in the circle next to the correct answer.

1. What do Joey's mom and dad both do?
   - Ⓐ They both fluff Joey's pillow.
   - Ⓑ They both kiss Joey good night.
   - Ⓒ They both help put away Joey's toys.

2. Joey's dad _____.
   - Ⓐ makes sure Joey brushes his teeth
   - Ⓑ buttons Joey's pajamas
   - Ⓒ reads Joey a story

3. Joey's mom _____.
   - Ⓐ reads Joey a story
   - Ⓑ fluffs Joey's pillow
   - Ⓒ makes sure Joey washes up

VOWEL SOUNDS

The letter y can have the long i sound.
Circle the words that have the long i sound.

1. Joey   2. story   3. dry   4. ready   5. sky

Name: _____

Compare and Contrast

WEEK 10
DAY 4

Read the story. Find out how Abe and Stella are the same and different.

> Abe and Stella like to read.
> They both get books from the library.
> They read about different things.
> Abe reads about real animals.
> He likes books about spiders the best.
> Stella reads books about friends.
> She likes funny books, too.
> Stella and Abe both read after supper.
> Abe stretches out on the floor.
> Stella sits in a big chair.

Fill in the circle next to the correct answer.

1. What is the same about Stella and Abe?
    Ⓐ They both read after supper.
    Ⓑ They both like to read funny books.
    Ⓒ They both read about animals.

2. How is Stella different from Abe?
    Ⓐ Stella likes to read, but Abe does not.
    Ⓑ Stella gets books from the library, but Abe does not.
    Ⓒ Stella reads funny stories, but Abe does not.

3. How is Abe different from Stella?
    Ⓐ Abe reads after supper, but Stella does not.
    Ⓑ Abe reads about spiders, but Stella does not.
    Ⓒ Abe reads about friends, but Stella does not.

ENDING SOUNDS

Look back at the story.
Circle six words that end in the same sound as <u>trees</u>.

Name: _____

Compare and Contrast

WEEK 10 DAY 5

Read the story. Find out how ducks and chickens are the same and different.

Ducks and chickens are birds.
They have feathers, and they can fly.
But ducks and chickens are different.
Chickens have pointed beaks.
Their feet are sharp.
Ducks have flat beaks.
Their feet have webs of skin.
Ducks use their feet to swim.
Ducks find food in the water.
Chickens cannot swim.
They use their beaks and feet to dig up food.

Fill in the circle next to the correct answer.

1. How are ducks and chickens the same?
   - Ⓐ They both dig for food.
   - Ⓑ They both have feathers.
   - Ⓒ They both have pointed beaks.

2. How is a duck different from a chicken?
   - Ⓐ A duck is a bird, but a chicken is not.
   - Ⓑ A duck can fly, but a chicken cannot.
   - Ⓒ A duck can swim, but a chicken cannot.

3. How is a chicken like a duck?
   - Ⓐ They both have flat beaks.
   - Ⓑ They both can fly.
   - Ⓒ They both can swim.

ENDING SOUNDS

Circle four words in the story that end with the same sound as peas.

WEEK 11

Fantasy and Reality

Students determine whether a story or specific information within it are fantastic or realistic.

DAY 1

Say: **This week we are going to practice telling the difference between what is make-believe and what can really happen. Another word for make-believe is** *fantasy.* **Things that can really happen are reality.** Give an example by telling something realistic and something fantastical, such as birds can fly and birds can fly over the moon. Then read the instructions at the top of the page aloud to focus students on the task. Read the story slowly, pausing after each sentence and allowing students to give a thumbs up when they hear something that can happen and a thumbs down when they hear something that is fantasy. Then direct students' attention to the first activity. Have them find and circle the key words in items 1 and 2. *(can really happen, make-believe)* Lead students in giving reasons for the correct and incorrect responses in item 3. Students may complete the sight words activity independently as you check their work.

DAY 2

Ask: **How do you know when something you read is make-believe?** (It can't really happen.) Read the instructions on the page aloud. Give a brief background about fireflies, if needed. Then instruct students to listen carefully as you read and to give a thumbs up when they hear something that can happen and a thumbs down when they hear something make-believe. If students disagree in their responses, stop reading and ask them to explain the reasons for their choices. After reading, lead students in completing the first activity. Let students complete the sight words activity with a partner. Check answers together.

DAY 3

Direct students' attention to the illustration. Ask: **What in this picture can really happen?** (For example: A cat can sit on a desk.) **Let's read the story and see if there are any make-believe events.** Read the instructions aloud. Read the story aloud as students follow. Then reread the story one sentence at a time, asking students to nod their heads when they hear something real and to shake their heads when they hear something that cannot happen. Guide students through the first activity. For item 3, call attention to the new key word, *true.* Let students complete the sight words activity with a partner. Check their answers together.

DAY 4

To review the reading skill, ask a student to name an animal. Let another student share a fact about that animal and a third student make up something fantastical about it. Then read the instructions aloud. Read the story. Instruct students to listen carefully and to indicate when they hear something that can happen. You may need to help students understand that the sentence "Then they raced like horses." is not make-believe. After reading, lead students through the first activity. Let them work individually on the sight words activity. Some students may find it useful to say the letters out loud as they write them.

DAY 5

Remind students of the skill. Read the instructions aloud. Then read the story as students follow along. They may enjoy reading with enthusiasm the words the clothing items say. Complete the activities as a class.

Name: _____

Fantasy and Reality WEEK 11 DAY 1

Read the story. Ask yourself, "What is make-believe and what can happen?"

It was just about midnight.
The moon was full and bright.
The people on the farm were asleep.
But the pigs were awake.
Papa Pig put on his cowboy hat.
He pulled on his boots, too.
Mama Pig put on her wig.
She snapped on her beads.
Crickets rubbed their wings.
They played a happy tune.
Papa Pig took Mama Pig's hand.
They danced in the light of the moon.

Fill in the circle next to the correct answer.

1. What in the story can really happen?
   Ⓐ Pigs can dance.
   Ⓑ The moon can be full and bright.
   Ⓒ Pigs like to wear boots.

2. What in the story is make-believe?
   Ⓐ A pig wears a wig.
   Ⓑ Crickets rub their wings.
   Ⓒ People live on a farm.

3. What is the best way to describe the story?
   Ⓐ It is a true story.
   Ⓑ It is a silly story.
   Ⓒ It is a news story.

SIGHT WORDS

Write the letters on the lines to spell the word <u>were</u>.

1. w___ re   2. ___ ere   3. we___ e   4. w___ ___ ___

© Evan-Moor Corp. • EMC 3451 • Daily Reading Comprehension

Name: _____

Fantasy and Reality **WEEK 11 DAY 2**

Read the story. Ask yourself, "What is make-believe and what can happen?"

Mia liked fireflies.
She did not harm them.
One night, Mia was lost.
It was too dark to see.
A cloud of fireflies flew to her.
The bugs wanted Mia to follow them.
They had very bright lights.
Their light turned the night into day.
Mia followed the fireflies.
They led Mia to her house.
She was happy to be home!

Fill in the circle next to the correct answer.

1. What in the story is make-believe?
   Ⓐ A girl is lost.
   Ⓑ The night is very dark.
   Ⓒ Fireflies know where a girl lives.

2. How does Mia find her way home?
   Ⓐ Mia uses a map.
   Ⓑ Mia follows fireflies.
   Ⓒ Mia has a light.

3. What in the story can really happen?
   Ⓐ Fireflies show a girl the way home.
   Ⓑ A girl gets lost in the dark.
   Ⓒ Fireflies turn the night into day.

SIGHT WORDS

Circle the two words that are the same.

1. has   2. was   3. his   4. had   5. was   6. wet

Name: _____

Fantasy and Reality

Read the story. Ask yourself, "What is make-believe and what can happen?"

Mazy the cat sat by Leo.
Leo tried to finish his homework.
But he was too tired.
Leo left the paper on his desk.
He gave his pet a quick pat.
Then he got into bed and fell asleep.
Mazy looked at Leo's homework.
She picked up a pencil.
She used her toes to count.
Mazy finished the page.
Then she looked at Leo and smiled.
She liked being Leo's friend.

Fill in the circle next to the correct answer.

1. What in the story is make-believe?
   Ⓐ A cat looks at a boy.
   Ⓑ A cat can do math.
   Ⓒ A boy does homework.

2. What in the story can really happen?
   Ⓐ A cat can like a boy.
   Ⓑ A cat can smile at a boy.
   Ⓒ A cat can write with a pencil.

3. What is true about cats?
   Ⓐ They can smile.
   Ⓑ They use their toes to count.
   Ⓒ They can be pets.

SIGHT WORDS

Circle the two words that are the same.

1. then 2. that 3. this 4. them 5. that

Name: _____

Fantasy and Reality

WEEK 11 DAY 4

Read the story. Ask yourself, "What is make-believe and what can happen?"

Kayla's birthday party was fun.
Everyone played pin the tail on the pony.
Then they raced like horses.
Later on, it was time for cake.
The cake was shaped like a horse.
Kayla's friends sang.
Then they yelled, "Make a wish!"
Kayla closed her eyes and made her wish.
With a big puff, Kayla blew out the candles.
Poof! A pony stood by her side.
The pony said, "I like your shoes, Kayla.
   Where can I get shoes that sparkle?"

Fill in the circle next to the correct answer.

1. What in the story can really happen?
   Ⓐ A girl can make a wish.
   Ⓑ A pony can talk like a person.
   Ⓒ A pony can wear people shoes.

2. Which sentence from the story is make-believe?
   Ⓐ "Then they raced like horses."
   Ⓑ "Kayla's friends sang."
   Ⓒ "Poof! A pony stood by her side."

3. What is the story about?
   Ⓐ A girl's birthday wish comes true.
   Ⓑ A birthday cake is shaped like a horse.
   Ⓒ A pony has a birthday party.

SIGHT WORDS

Write the letters on the lines to spell the word <u>where</u>.

1. wher___   2. ___ ___ere   3. w___ ___ ___ ___

Name: _____

WEEK 11
Fantasy and Reality **DAY 5**

Read the story. Ask yourself, "What is make-believe and what can happen?"

Jake had to change his clothes.
So he tugged off his shirt.
He tossed the shirt across his room.
"Ouch!" cried the shirt.
Then Jake kicked off his shoes.
They flew through the air.
And they landed with a thump.
The shoes yelled, "Be careful!"
Jake pulled off a sock.
He rolled it into a ball.
"Wham!" The sock landed in a trash basket.
"Hey! It's dark in here!" shouted the sock.

Fill in the circle next to the correct answer.

1. What in the story can really happen?
   Ⓐ Shoes can yell.
   Ⓑ A shirt can cry.
   Ⓒ A boy can throw his sock.

2. What in the story is make-believe?
   Ⓐ A boy kicks off his shoes.
   Ⓑ A sock does not like the dark.
   Ⓒ A boy tosses his shirt.

3. What is true about clothes?
   Ⓐ Clothes cry.
   Ⓑ Clothes get hurt.
   Ⓒ Clothes get dirty.

SIGHT WORDS

Circle the word that correctly completes the sentence.

Look at the clothes. (They   Them) are dirty.

WEEK 12

Prediction

With Prediction, students use clues from a story and prior knowledge to predict what will happen next. Students understand that good predictions follow logically from the events of the story.

DAY 1

Tell students that this week they will be practicing the reading skill called *Prediction*. Say: **To predict means to make a good guess about what may happen next. Good readers pay close attention to what characters say and do. They use these clues to predict what will probably happen next.** Read the instructions at the top of the page aloud. Then read the story aloud as students follow along, reading the words they know. After reading, slowly guide students through the first activity. Let them consider each answer choice and determine which is supported by the text. Call attention to the word meanings activity. Say: **A story often gives clues about what words mean. Let's find the word *spray* in the story and read the sentence.** After doing so, let students circle their responses and indicate their answer choices with a show of hands.

DAY 2

Review the skill of *Prediction* and the importance of reading for clues as to what will probably happen next. Direct students' attention to the illustration, and identify the main character as Sara. Read the instructions aloud to focus students on the task. Then read the story one sentence at a time, with students reading the sentence after you. After reading, guide students in completing the first activity. Continually refer them back to the story for clues that help determine the correct responses. Do the word meanings activity together. Have students first locate the word *wavy* in the story and read it in context.

DAY 3

Remind students of the prediction about Sara made on Day 2. (She will probably go somewhere special.) Ask students to recall the story clues that helped them make the prediction. (Sara is all dressed up; she is wearing ribbons in her hair.) Say: **Sometimes when you read, you already know things that will help you make a good prediction. Today's story is about a boy named Jared who is making a tower. You can use what you know about stacking things to help you predict what will happen next.** Read the story aloud. After reading, lead students through the first activity, carefully considering each answer choice. Invite students to share their experiences regarding items 1 and 3. Complete the word meanings activity together. Let students explain why some objects can be stacked and some objects can't.

DAY 4

Tell students that today's story is about a horse. Read the instructions aloud. Then read the story as students follow along. After reading, help students complete the first activity, relying on story clues and prior knowledge. Then ask students to describe a meadow to a partner, based on what was read in the story. Let students circle their answers, and check them for accuracy.

DAY 5

Invite students to tell a partner what they know about making predictions while reading. Share some responses. Then read the instructions aloud. Ask students to listen carefully to the story as you read. After reading, lead students in completing the first activity. Encourage students to refer to story clues for help. Let students do the word meanings activity independently. Then ask them to hold up the number of fingers that indicate their answers.

Name: _____

Prediction WEEK 12 DAY 1

Read the story. Ask yourself, "What will probably happen next?"

The skunk wants to get away from the dog.
But the skunk has short legs.
It cannot run fast.
So the skunk tries to scare the dog.
The skunk hisses and growls.
But the dog does not move.
The skunk pounds its foot.
The sound does not scare the dog.
Then the skunk lifts its tail.
The skunk shoots stinky spray at the dog's face.
The dog's eyes hurt.
The dog cannot see.

Fill in the circle next to the correct answer.

1. What will probably happen next?
   Ⓐ The skunk will laugh at the dog.
   Ⓑ The skunk will get away.
   Ⓒ The skunk will hiss and pound.

2. How will the skunk scare the dog?
   Ⓐ by hissing
   Ⓑ by pounding
   Ⓒ by shooting stinky spray

3. What will probably happen the next time the dog sees the skunk?
   Ⓐ The dog will spray the skunk.
   Ⓑ The dog will run away.
   Ⓒ The skunk will run fast.

WORD MEANINGS

Circle the picture of a spray of water.

1.    2.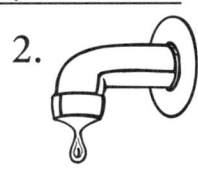

Name: _____

WEEK 12
Prediction **DAY 2**

Read the story. Ask yourself, "What will probably happen next?"

Sara likes to wear jeans and tee shirts.
But today she is all dressed up.
Her dress is full and fluffy.
It nearly covers her legs.
Sara's socks are white and lacy.
Her shoes are shiny and pink.
Sara always wears ponytails with rubber bands.
But today her hair is long and wavy.
Sara's mom put ribbons in Sara's hair.

Fill in the circle next to the correct answer.

1. What will Sara probably do next?
   Ⓐ Sara will play soccer.
   Ⓑ Sara will go to sleep.
   Ⓒ Sara will go somewhere special.

2. How will Sara probably wear her hair tomorrow?
   Ⓐ She will wear ribbons.
   Ⓑ She will wear ponytails.
   Ⓒ She will wear it wavy.

3. Which sentence tells that Sara is dressed up?
   Ⓐ Her dress is full and fluffy.
   Ⓑ Sara likes to wear jeans.
   Ⓒ Sara wears ponytails.

WORD MEANINGS

Circle the picture that goes with the words.

1. wavy hair

2. lacy sock

Name: _____

Prediction WEEK 12 DAY 3

Read the story. Ask yourself, "What will probably happen next?"

Jared wants to make a tower.
He is using things that he finds in his yard.
Jared starts by laying two bricks on the grass.
Then he stacks some flat rocks on the bricks.
Jared piles more bricks on top of the rocks.
Then he puts on a few twigs.
The tower is getting tall.
Jared finds some pieces of wood.
He places one piece on top of another.
He puts the biggest board on top.
The tower starts to tip.

Fill in the circle next to the correct answer.

1. What will probably happen next?
   Ⓐ The tower will fall.
   Ⓑ The tower will stand.
   Ⓒ The tower will be taller than a tree.

2. What is the story about?
   Ⓐ things that are in a boy's yard
   Ⓑ rocks and bricks
   Ⓒ a boy making a tower

3. What will Jared probably do the next time he makes a tower?
   Ⓐ He will place pine cones on top of the flat rocks.
   Ⓑ He will place the biggest board near the bottom.
   Ⓒ He will stack heavy bricks on the top.

WORD MEANINGS

Circle all that you can <u>stack</u>.

1. pennies   2. books   3. balls   4. cats

Name: _____

Prediction WEEK 12 DAY 4

Read the story. Ask yourself, "What will probably happen next?"

The horse liked to run in the meadow.
One day, the horse was put inside a fence.
The horse wanted to be free.
It called as loudly as it could.
No one came to let the horse go.
The horse was upset!
It kicked out with its back legs.
Then the horse kicked the fence.
Its feet were strong.
The fence was old and made of wood.

Fill in the circle next to the correct answer.

1. What will probably happen next?
   Ⓐ The horse will go under the fence.
   Ⓑ The horse will go to sleep.
   Ⓒ The horse will kick down the fence.

2. What will the horse probably do if it kicks down the fence?
   Ⓐ run away
   Ⓑ stay inside the fence
   Ⓒ get help to fix the fence

3. Which one tells about the horse?
   Ⓐ The horse is funny.
   Ⓑ The horse is a good pet.
   Ⓒ The horse is mad.

WORD MEANINGS

Circle the picture that shows a <u>meadow</u>.

1.    2.    3.

Name: _____

Prediction **WEEK 12 DAY 5**

Read the story. Ask yourself, "What will probably happen next?"

Long ago, the King of Everything had a cat.
The king loved his cat more than anything.
The cat lived a very good life.
Its toys filled a room in the castle.
It ate the freshest fish from the sea.
And it slept on a pillow stuffed with duck feathers.
That pillow sat on a gold chair next to the king.
The cat had everything except for one thing.
The cat did not have a name.
The king called for the smartest people he knew.

Fill in the circle next to the correct answer.

1. What will the king probably do next?
   Ⓐ ask the smart people to play with the cat
   Ⓑ ask the smart people to name the cat
   Ⓒ ask the smart people to feed the cat

2. Which word best describes the cat?
   Ⓐ friendly
   Ⓑ smart
   Ⓒ spoiled

3. What is something the king will probably do for his cat?
   Ⓐ buy the cat more toys
   Ⓑ order the cat to wear a collar
   Ⓒ make the cat sleep outside

WORD MEANINGS

Circle what means the same as everything.

1. some   2. a little   3. all   4. none

WEEK 13

Main Idea and Details

Students read to understand the central message of a passage or story. They also monitor their comprehension of important details.

DAY 1
Tell students that this week they will practice the reading skill *Main Idea and Details*. Say: **Every story has a main idea, which is what the story is mostly about. Knowing the main idea helps you understand what you are reading.** Read the instructions at the top of the page aloud. Ask: **Do poems have a main idea?** (Yes. Every poem tells about something.) Read the first stanza of the poem aloud as students follow along. Pause and ask students to tell the main idea in their own words. (Wind can be strong.) Do the same after reading the second stanza. (Wind can move softly.) Guide students in completing the first activity. For item 1, help students differentiate the details about the main idea (B and C) from the main idea (A). To complete the phonics activity, reread the poem. Students may find it helpful to work with a partner.

DAY 2
Review the skill. Then direct students' attention to the illustration, and identify the boy as Harry. Read the instructions aloud. Read the story as students follow along. Then help students differentiate the main idea and details by making a web on the board. Ask students who the story is about, and write the word *Harry* and circle it. Then ask students to recall details about Harry. List those details on lines extending from the name *Harry*. Refer to the details on the board when guiding students to determine the main idea (item 1) in the first activity. (The details tell about the main idea—Harry plays in puddles.) Erase Harry's circled name and replace it with the main idea. Leave the web on the board to use as a review for Day 3. Help students complete the remainder of the page.

DAY 3
Use the web from Day 2 to review the main idea and supporting details. Then read the instructions on page 85 aloud. Read the story aloud as students follow along, reading the words they know. After reading, guide students through the first activity. After completing item 1, ask students to tell a partner one detail they remember about Rusty and the job she does. Allow time for sharing responses. Then complete items 2 and 3, helping students determine why only one choice is correct and the others are not. Lead students in doing the phonics activity together.

DAY 4
Recall that the main idea tells what a story is about and details tell about the main idea. Direct students' attention to the illustration, and identify the main character as Cody. Read the instructions aloud and invite students to read along with you. After reading, ask: **Is the rake really a snake?** (no) **Is it a sword?** (no) Guide students through the first activity. Identify item 1 as finding the main idea. Identify items 2 and 3 as details that tell about Cody. Then complete the page together.

DAY 5
Review the reading skill *Main Idea and Details*. Read the instructions aloud, and then read the story to students as they listen. After reading, lead students through the first activity. Students may work in pairs to do the phonics activity. Check their answers as a class.

Name: _____

Main Idea and Details **WEEK 13 DAY 1**

Read the poem. Ask yourself, "What is this poem about?"

The wind is air that moves.
The wind can be strong.
It rocks a boat on the sea.
And with a loud gust,
It bends a big tree.

The wind is air that moves.
The wind can be soft.
It takes a kite across the sky.
And with a light push,
It makes the dust fly.

Fill in the circle next to the correct answer.

1. What is the poem about?
   Ⓐ what the wind can do
   Ⓑ what the wind can do to a kite
   Ⓒ what the wind can do to a tree

2. Which sentence tells about a soft wind?
   Ⓐ A soft wind can move a boat.
   Ⓑ A soft wind can bend a tree.
   Ⓒ A soft wind can make a kite fly.

3. Which one tells about wind?
   Ⓐ Wind is always strong.
   Ⓑ Wind can be strong or soft.
   Ⓒ Wind is always soft.

RHYMING WORDS

Read the first part of the poem. Circle the two words that rhyme.
Read the second part. Circle the two words that rhyme.

© Evan-Moor Corp. • EMC 3451 • Daily Reading Comprehension

Name: _____

Main Idea and Details

WEEK 13 DAY 2

Read the story. Ask yourself, "What is this story about?"

Harry likes to play outside after it rains.
He puts on his yellow rain jacket.
Then he pulls on his shiny green boots.
The boots look like smiling frogs.
The red front door slams with a bang.
Harry races outside.
He runs to a big puddle.
Harry thinks his boots are jumping frogs.
Splash go his feet!
Splash go two shiny frogs into the water!

Fill in the circle next to the correct answer.

1. What is the story about?
   Ⓐ Harry gets dressed.
   Ⓑ Harry has two pet frogs.
   Ⓒ Harry likes to play in puddles.

2. What does Harry do in the puddles?
   Ⓐ He puts frogs in them.
   Ⓑ He throws rocks into them.
   Ⓒ He jumps in them.

3. Which one shows Harry's boots?

VOWEL SOUNDS

Circle the words that have the same vowel sound you hear in <u>boot</u>.

1. book   2. soon   3. room   4. look

Name: _____

Main Idea and Details

WEEK 13 DAY 3

Read the story. Ask yourself, "What is this story about?"

> Rusty the dog has a job.
> She takes care of sheep.
> Rusty creeps low in the grass.
> She watches the sheep closely.
> She does things to keep the sheep together.
> Rusty stares at the sheep.
> She runs around the sheep and barks.
> The sheep stay together.
> Then the sheep are safe.
> The sheep need Rusty.

Fill in the circle next to the correct answer.

1. What is the story about?
   Ⓐ a sheep named Rusty
   Ⓑ a dog named Rusty
   Ⓒ a sheep that can creep

2. What job does Rusty do?
   Ⓐ Rusty runs and eats.
   Ⓑ Rusty creeps in the grass.
   Ⓒ Rusty keeps sheep safe.

3. Which one describes Rusty?
   Ⓐ She does her job.
   Ⓑ She eats grass.
   Ⓒ She sleeps a lot.

BEGINNING SOUNDS

Circle the two letters at the beginning of each word that together spell one sound.

1. sheep   2. them   3. while

© Evan-Moor Corp. • EMC 3451 • Daily Reading Comprehension

Name: _____

Main Idea and Details

WEEK 13 DAY 4

Read the story. Ask yourself, "What is this story about?"

Cody's job is to rake the leaves.
Cody wiggles the rake.
The rake is a snake.

Next, Cody pushes the rake up and back.
He is in a boat.
He paddles with the rake across a lake.

Then, the rake is a sword.
Cody fights a dragon.

Finally, Cody pulls the rake through the grass.
He makes a pile of the leaves.
Now the rake is just a rake.

Fill in the circle next to the correct answer.

1. What is the story about?
   Ⓐ a boy who likes to pretend
   Ⓑ a boy who is brave
   Ⓒ a boy who has a pet snake

2. Which one tells about Cody?
   Ⓐ He works quickly.
   Ⓑ He plays before he works.
   Ⓒ He has many chores.

3. What does Cody do with the rake that is make-believe?
   Ⓐ He gathers leaves.
   Ⓑ He rakes the grass.
   Ⓒ He paddles a boat.

RHYMING WORDS

Circle two words in the story that rhyme with <u>rake</u>.

Name: _____

Main Idea and Details

WEEK 13 DAY 5

Read the story. Ask yourself, "What is this story about?"

July was a hot month.
So Jessie had a swim party.
She invited three girls who lived nearby.
Jessie made a snack to eat after swimming.
She mixed some dip to go with chips.
The sky was sunny when the party began.
The girls tossed a ball in the pool.
But then the sky turned dark.
The rain came down hard.
The girls quickly climbed out of the pool.
It was time for chips and dip.

Fill in the circle next to the correct answer.

1. What is the story about?
   Ⓐ a girl and her swim party
   Ⓑ a sudden rainstorm
   Ⓒ a hot summer day

2. What was a problem that happened in the story?
   Ⓐ It started to rain.
   Ⓑ Jessie forgot to make a snack.
   Ⓒ The pool had a leak.

3. What does Jessie do to get ready for the swim party?
   Ⓐ She makes chips.
   Ⓑ She fills the pool with water.
   Ⓒ She makes a snack.

VOWEL SOUNDS

Circle the letter or letters in each word that spell the long e sound.

1. be   2. three   3. feet   4. eat   5. party

© Evan-Moor Corp. • EMC 3451 • Daily Reading Comprehension

87

WEEK 14

Who, What, and Where

Students read to determine "who" (the main character), "what" (the main character's actions), and "where" (the setting).

DAY 1
Write *Who*, *What*, and *Where* on the board. (Leave the headings there for the remainder of the week.) Point to each word as you tell students they will practice finding *Who* the main character of a story is, *What* the character does, and *Where* the story takes place. Students are likely to be familiar with the nursery rhyme "Mary Had a Little Lamb." If so, tell them they will read the true story about Mary and her lamb. Then read the instructions at the top of the page aloud. Read the story as students listen. After reading, guide students in completing the first activity. For item 1, help them understand that this story has two main characters. Recap by filling in information about the story under the headings on the board. Let students complete the sight words activity independently.

DAY 2
Refer students to the *Who, What, Where* information on the board from Day 1 and review the skill. Then direct their attention to the story, and read the instructions aloud. Ask students to listen as you read and to picture the story in their minds. After reading, allow a few students to share what they pictured. Then lead students through the first activity. For item 1, encourage them to explain why B is the correct answer. After the first activity, recap the story by adding story information under the *Who, What, Where* headings on the board. Instruct students to complete the sight words activity independently.

DAY 3
Refer to yesterday's *Who, What, Where* information on the board to review the skill. Then direct students' attention to the story, and read the instructions aloud. Read the story as students follow along. After reading, say: **Put up your fingers to show how many main characters this story has.** (two) Recap the story by adding to the headings on the board. Guide students in completing the first activity. Allow students to do the sight words activity with a partner, reading the words out loud.

DAY 4
Instruct students to review yesterday's story information with a partner, using the three headings on the board. Then direct their attention to the story, and read the instructions aloud. Read the story aloud as students follow long, reading the words they know. After reading, recap the story as on previous days. Complete the activities together.

DAY 5
Refer students to the headings on the board and ask them to say out loud which one tells the main character of a story. (Who) Remind students that the main character can be an animal. Read the instructions aloud, and then read the story one sentence at a time. Instruct students to read each sentence after you. Complete the first activity with students, asking them to read specific story sentences that support the correct answers. Complete the sight words activity together.

Name: _____

Who, What, and Where

WEEK 14 DAY 1

Read the story. Ask yourself, "Who? What? Where?"

A long time ago, Mary had a little lamb.
The lamb followed her everywhere.
Step, step, step went Mary.
Clop, clop, clop went the lamb.
One day, the lamb followed Mary to school.
Mary hid the lamb under her chair.
The teacher called Mary to the front of the room.
It was Mary's turn to read.
Step, step, step went Mary.
Clop, clop, clop went the lamb!

Today, many children sing a song.
The song tells about Mary and her little lamb.

Fill in the circle next to the correct answer.

1. What is the story about?
   Ⓐ a lamb
   Ⓑ a girl named Mary
   Ⓒ Mary and her lamb

2. What does the lamb do one day?
   Ⓐ The lamb eats grass.
   Ⓑ The lamb follows Mary to school.
   Ⓒ The lamb goes with Mary to a store.

3. Where does the story take place?
   Ⓐ on a farm
   Ⓑ at a school
   Ⓒ under a chair

SIGHT WORDS

Write the letters on the lines to spell the word <u>under</u>.

1. un___ ___   2. ___ ___der   3. und___ ___

Daily Reading Comprehension • EMC 3451 • © Evan-Moor Corp.

Name: _____

Who, What, and Where

WEEK 14 DAY 2

Read the story. Ask yourself, "Who? What? Where?"

Grandma and Rey like making cookies together.
Rey pours and Grandma mixes.
They both scoop dough onto spoons.
Rey likes to drop the dough onto a cookie sheet.
They clean up while the cookies bake.
Rey stacks the bowl and spoons in the sink.
Grandma wipes the table.
The cat licks the sugar that spilled.
Rey can hardly wait for the timer to ring.
Making cookies is fun.
But eating them is better!

Fill in the circle next to the correct answer.

1. Who is the story about?
   Ⓐ Rey
   Ⓑ Rey and his grandma
   Ⓒ Grandma

2. What are the people in the story doing?
   Ⓐ eating cookies
   Ⓑ buying cookies
   Ⓒ baking cookies

3. Where does the story probably take place?
   Ⓐ in a kitchen
   Ⓑ in a stove
   Ⓒ in a bedroom

SIGHT WORDS

Write the letters on the lines to spell the word <u>could</u>.

1. ___ould   2. cou___ ___   3. c___ ___ld

Name: _____

Who, What, and Where **WEEK 14 DAY 3**

Read the story. Ask yourself, "Who? What? Where?"

The kids laughed while they played.
Carl kicked the ground with his feet.
Then he stuck out his legs.
His swing went higher and higher.
Carl held the chains and leaned back.
He saw the sun peeking through the trees.
Carl's friend Jade climbed up to the slide.
She liked the way the slide twisted.
Jade bumped into the sides as she slid.
Then she landed in a pile of soft sand.

Fill in the circle next to the correct answer.

1. Who is playing with Carl?
   Ⓐ his sister Jade
   Ⓑ his mother Jade
   Ⓒ his friend Jade

2. What does Jade do?
   Ⓐ She makes her swing go high.
   Ⓑ She goes down a slide.
   Ⓒ She sees the sun peek through the trees.

3. Where does the story probably take place?
   Ⓐ in a store
   Ⓑ in a park
   Ⓒ in a classroom

SIGHT WORDS

Circle the two words that are the same.

1. were   2. went   3. want   4. went   5. where

Daily Reading Comprehension • EMC 3451 • © Evan-Moor Corp.

Name: _____

Who, What, and Where

WEEK 14 DAY 4

Read the story. Ask yourself, "Who? What? Where?"

A zoo vet takes care of all kinds of animals.
Some of the animals fly.
Some swing from trees.
And some kick with big feet.
All of the animals in a zoo are wild.
So a zoo vet must be careful.
The vet gives a sick animal a shot.
The shot makes the animal fall asleep.
Then the vet checks the animal.
She must work quickly.
She needs to finish before the animal wakes up!

Fill in the circle next to the correct answer.

1. What is the job of a zoo vet?
   Ⓐ to help sick animals in a zoo
   Ⓑ to feed zoo animals
   Ⓒ to clean the cages of zoo animals

2. Who is the story about?
   Ⓐ someone who takes care of pets
   Ⓑ someone who takes care of zoo animals
   Ⓒ someone who takes care of people

3. Where does the story take place?
   Ⓐ in a tree
   Ⓑ in a zoo
   Ⓒ in a jungle

SIGHT WORDS

Circle the word that correctly completes the sentence.

The sick animal (must   mist) be taken to a vet.

92 Daily Reading Comprehension • EMC 3451 • © Evan-Moor Corp.

Name: _____

Who, What, and Where — WEEK 14 DAY 5

Read the story. Ask yourself, "Who? What? Where?"

Snails live on land and in water.
A snail's body is soft.
It has a head and one long foot.
The foot makes a trail of slime.
A snail moves by gliding along on the slime.
It can even crawl upside down on its slime.
All snails have hard shells, too.
A snail can pull its body inside its shell.
Then the snail's soft body is safe.

Fill in the circle next to the correct answer.

1. What is the story about?
   Ⓐ where snails live
   Ⓑ the way snails move
   Ⓒ some facts about snails

2. Where do snails live?
   Ⓐ in space
   Ⓑ in water and on land
   Ⓒ on land only

3. What is true about snails?
   Ⓐ Snails can crawl upside down.
   Ⓑ Snails have two feet.
   Ⓒ Snails have hard bodies.

SIGHT WORDS

Circle the word that correctly completes the sentence.

Snails (live   left) inside their shells in the winter.

Daily Reading Comprehension • EMC 3451 • © Evan-Moor Corp.

WEEK 15

Sequence

Students practice Sequence to determine the order of events or steps in a process.

DAY 1

Tell students that this week they will practice the reading skill called *Sequence*. Say: **Sequence is the order in which you do something. Writers use signal words that help the reader understand the order.** Read the instructions at the top of the page aloud. Ask students what the steps will tell how to make. (a food face) Instruct students to listen for signal words as they listen to you read the story aloud. Read the story a second time slowly. Have students raise their hands when they hear a signal word. Instruct them to circle each signal word. *(First, Next, Then, Last)* Guide students through the first activity. Then read the directions for the word meanings activity together. Say: **Good readers look back to the story for clues about what words mean.** Let students find the word *form* in the story and read it in context. Then help them determine the correct response.

DAY 2

Review the skill of *Sequence* and the importance of signal words. Remind students that signal words are often the first word in a sentence. Say: **We are going to read a story that tells the order in which a girl does things to get ready to bat during a baseball game.** Have students search the story for five signal words and circle them. *(First, Then, Next, Then, Finally)* Then read the instructions aloud. Read the story as students follow along. After reading, have students stand and act out what Kelly does in order. Then guide students to complete the first activity by first circling the key words. *(first, before, After)* Do the word meanings activity together. Remind students that action words tell what someone does. Read sentences five, six, and eight. Have students determine which are action words by acting them out. *(tugs, rubs, wiggles)*

DAY 3

Direct students' attention to the story, and read the instructions aloud. Then say: **This story is divided into five steps. The steps tell the order, or sequence, for making a picture.** Read the story as students follow along. To help them understand the five steps, read them again and have students act them out, pretending to make a soap bubble picture. Then guide students in completing the first activity. Read item 1. Then have students find step 1 in the story, point to it, and read it. Read item 2. Then ask students to find the word *blow* in the story and read that step. Then ask students to find the word *spill* in the story and read that step. Then complete the word meanings activity together.

DAY 4

Review *Sequence* as the order in which things happen. Read the instructions aloud. Say: **Let's find and circle the signal words to help us remember each step.** *(First, Next, Then, Now)* Read the story with students. After reading, complete the first activity, helping students to locate signal words in the story to assist them in finding the answers. Then direct students' attention to the word meanings activity and explain the diagram. If needed, help students look back at the story for the answer.

DAY 5

Remind students of the skill. Then read the instructions aloud. Say: **Look through the story. Do you see any signal words that tell the order in which things happen?** (no) **This means you will have to listen even more carefully to what happens. It may help to picture the story in your mind.** Read the story slowly and, if helpful, read it a second time. Then lead students in completing the first activity. Help students decide on key words in the items and find them in the story as an aide for locating the answers. Do the word meanings activity together. First read the sentence in the story containing the word *dashed*.

Name: _____

Sequence **WEEK 15 DAY 1**

Read the directions. Remember the steps for making a food face.

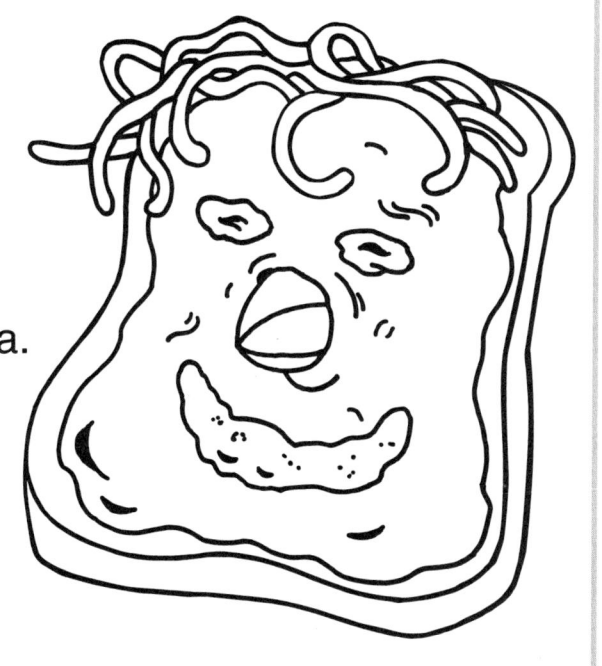

You can make a food face.
It is easy to do.
First, take one slice of bread.
Next, spread it with peanut butter.
Then, make eyes with raisins.
Form a nose with the tip of a banana.
Shape a smile with red jelly.
Last, pull some cheese into strings.
Place the cheese to look like hair.
There it is!
You have a face that is good to eat!

Fill in the circle next to the correct answer.

1. What is a <u>food face</u> in the story?
   Ⓐ food that is stuck on your face
   Ⓑ food that looks like a face
   Ⓒ food that is made with raisins

2. What is the first thing you do with the bread?
   Ⓐ spread it with peanut butter
   Ⓑ place cheese to look like hair
   Ⓒ make a smile with jelly

3. What do you do after making a smile on the bread?
   Ⓐ make a banana nose
   Ⓑ make raisin eyes
   Ⓒ make cheese look like hair

WORD MEANINGS

Circle something you can <u>form</u>.

   1. water   2. grass   3. clay

Name: _____

Sequence — **WEEK 15 DAY 2**

Read the story. Remember how the girl gets ready to bat.

> Kelly plays baseball during the summer.
> Her team cheers when Kelly goes to bat.
> She stands tall as she walks to the plate.
> She gets ready.
> First, she tugs up her pants.
> Then, she rubs her hands together.
> Next, she takes two practice swings with the bat.
> Then, Kelly wiggles her fingers on the bat.
> Finally, she stands still and stares at the pitcher.
> Kelly is ready to get a hit.

Fill in the circle next to the correct answer.

1. What is the first thing Kelly does to get ready to bat?
   Ⓐ She tugs up her pants.
   Ⓑ She stares at the pitcher.
   Ⓒ She walks to the plate.

2. What does Kelly do before she wiggles her fingers?
   Ⓐ She takes two practice swings.
   Ⓑ She stares at the pitcher.
   Ⓒ She stands still.

3. After Kelly wiggles her fingers, she _____.
   Ⓐ stares at the pitcher
   Ⓑ tugs up her pants
   Ⓒ rubs her hands together

WORD MEANINGS

Circle three action words in the story that tell what Kelly <u>does</u> to get ready.

Name: _____

Sequence WEEK 15 DAY 3

Read the directions. Remember the steps for making a soap bubble picture.

You use soap for washing.
You can use soap to make some art, too.
Follow the steps below to make a soap bubble picture.

1. Mix some dish soap and water in a cup.
2. Place the cup on a sheet of colored paper.
3. Put a straw into the cup.
   Blow to make a lot of bubbles.
4. Blow until bubbles spill onto the paper.
   The bubbles will pop and make bubble shapes.
5. Move the cup to other parts of the paper.
   Make more bubble shapes until you like the picture.

Fill in the circle next to the correct answer.

1. What do you need for step 1?
   Ⓐ a sheet of colored paper
   Ⓑ a straw and bubbles
   Ⓒ dish soap, water, and a cup

2. You first blow into the cup with a straw in step _____.
   Ⓐ 5
   Ⓑ 3
   Ⓒ 4

3. What happens when the bubbles spill onto the paper?
   Ⓐ They pop and make bubble shapes.
   Ⓑ They make more bubbles.
   Ⓒ They make square shapes.

WORD MEANINGS

What does the word <u>spill</u> in step 4 mean?

1. to crush   2. to fall out   3. to pop

© Evan-Moor Corp. • EMC 3451 • Daily Reading Comprehension

Name: _____

WEEK 15 Sequence **DAY 4**

Read the story. Remember each step in how a frog grows.

How does a frog grow?
First, it is a tiny egg.
The egg is in a pond.
Next, a tadpole comes out of the egg.
A tadpole is just a head and a tail.
It breathes with gills.
Then, the tadpole grows big legs.
The tail goes away.
Now it is a frog.
It breathes with lungs.
It hops out of the water.
The frog is hungry for bugs.

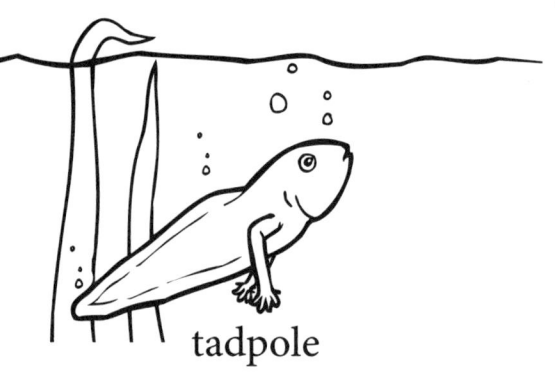
tadpole

frog

Fill in the circle next to the correct answer.

1. How does a frog begin?
   Ⓐ as an egg
   Ⓑ as a tadpole
   Ⓒ as gills

2. What does the egg become next?
   Ⓐ a frog
   Ⓑ a tadpole
   Ⓒ a tail

3. What can a frog do?
   Ⓐ wag its tail
   Ⓑ hop with legs
   Ⓒ breathe with gills

WORD MEANINGS

Circle the word that names what the tadpole uses to <u>breathe</u>.

Name: _____

Sequence — WEEK 15, DAY 5

Read the story. Ask yourself, "What happens first, next, and last?"

David tripped over his cat.
David fell and so did his backpack.
His homework spilled onto the floor.
The cat yowled and dashed away.
The dog woke up and chased the cat.
The dog ran over David's homework.
Its claws made a lot of holes!
The cat jumped onto the table.
The dog tried to reach the cat.
A glass of juice tipped over.
Juice dripped onto David's homework.
What a mess!

Fill in the circle next to the correct answer.

1. What does the cat do after David trips over it?
   Ⓐ It jumps onto the table.
   Ⓑ It yowls.
   Ⓒ It knocks over the juice.

2. Which of these does the dog do first?
   Ⓐ It chases the cat.
   Ⓑ It knocks over the juice.
   Ⓒ It runs over David's homework.

3. What is the last thing that happens to David's homework?
   Ⓐ Juice drips on it.
   Ⓑ It gets holes in it.
   Ⓒ It tears apart.

WORD MEANINGS

Circle how the cat moved when it <u>dashed</u>.

1. The cat walked.   2. The cat jumped.   3. The cat ran.

WEEK 16

Compare and Contrast

Students practice Compare and Contrast *by looking at the similarities and differences between two people or things.*

DAY 1
Say: **This week we will practice the reading skill of *Compare and Contrast*, or telling how people or things are the same (comparing) and how they are different (contrasting).** Direct students' attention to the illustration, and identify the two main characters as Kia, on the left, and Yuki. On the board write *Yuki* and *Kia* as headings for two columns. Read the instructions at the top of the page aloud, and then read the story to students. Read the story a second time, pausing after each sentence to ask students if you should write something under one of the girls' names. After compiling the two lists, circle the facts that tell differences between the two girls. Then guide students in completing the first activity. Reread sentences in the story to verify answer choices. Complete the phonics activity together.

DAY 2
Review the skill. Tell students that they are going to read about two kinds of trees. Then read the instructions aloud. Say: **This story has two parts. The first part tells about one kind of tree. Let's read about that kind of tree.** After reading the first part, say: **Now let's read about another kind of tree.** Read the second part. Then make a Venn diagram that shows the facts read. Guide students through the first activity, referring to the Venn diagram as needed. Ask students to complete the phonics activity independently. Allow time for sharing of responses.

DAY 3
Remind students of the skill. Say: **Today we are going to read a story about two brothers who are eating spaghetti.** Read the instructions aloud, and then read the story as students follow along. Read the story again, making a Venn diagram of the facts. Keep the information simple. *(Cody—slurps, red nose; Jud—twirls, messy face, messy glass; Both—like spaghetti, messy eaters)* Then lead students in completing the first activity, circling the key words in an item before answering it. *(same, different, different)* Refer to the Venn diagram as needed. For the phonics activity, first isolate the vowel sound in *mouse* and have students repeat it after you. Slowly reread the first five sentences in the story. Ask students to raise their hands when they hear a word with the same vowel sound heard in *mouse*.

DAY 4
Tell students that today they will read about spiders and insects. Read the instructions aloud. Then direct students' attention to the illustration. Say: **Good readers look at the pictures to help them understand what they are reading.** Read the story aloud as students follow along, reading the words they know. Pause at appropriate sentences for students to use the illustration as an aide. After reading, have students label the spider and the insect in the picture. Then guide students in completing the first activity. Call attention to the key word *and* in item 2 before determining the answer. Students may complete the phonics activity with a partner.

DAY 5
Direct students' attention to the illustration, and have them identify the two balls. Read the instructions aloud. Read the story as students follow along. Use a Venn diagram to record facts learned about the two kinds of balls. As you lead students through the first activity, find and circle the key words in each item. *(both, different, different)* Say: **Think about what we read and wrote in the Venn diagram as you choose the correct answers.** Complete the phonics activity together. Have students read the words out loud and raise their hands when the short /a/ sound is heard.

Name: _____

Compare and Contrast — WEEK 16 DAY 1

Read the story. Look for ways that Yuki and Kia are the same and different.

Yuki and Kia are in second grade.
They both are learning handwriting.
But the girls go to different schools.
The kids at Yuki's school wear uniforms.
They change their shoes inside their school.
Every student at Yuki's school does a chore.
The kids at Kia's school mostly wear jeans.
They do not change their shoes at school.
The kids can offer to do a job in the classroom.
Yuki goes to school in Japan.
Kia's school is in the United States.

Fill in the circle next to the correct answer.

1. How are the schools different?
   Ⓐ Yuki's school is in the United States, but Kia's is in Japan.
   Ⓑ Yuki's school teaches handwriting, but Kia's school does not.
   Ⓒ Everyone does a chore at Yuki's school, but not at Kia's.

2. Yuki and Kia are alike because _____.
   Ⓐ they go to the same school
   Ⓑ they are in second grade
   Ⓒ they wear jeans to school

3. How is Kia's school different from Yuki's school?
   Ⓐ At Kia's school, the kids wear jeans, but at Yuki's school they do not.
   Ⓑ At Kia's school, the kids wear uniforms, but at Yuki's school they do not.
   Ⓒ Kia's school is in Japan, but Yuki's school is not.

COMPOUND WORDS

Draw a line between the two words that make up each word below.

1. classroom   2. handwriting   3. everyone

© Evan-Moor Corp. • EMC 3451 • Daily Reading Comprehension

Compare and Contrast — WEEK 16, DAY 2

Read the story. Find out how the trees are the same and how they are different.

All trees have green leaves.
Some trees lose their leaves at one time.
Their green leaves turn brown in the fall.
Then they all drop off.
Their branches no longer have leaves.
New leaves will grow next spring.

Some trees stay green all year round.
Those trees are called evergreens.
Evergreens lose only a few leaves at one time.
New leaves quickly take their place.

Fill in the circle next to the correct answer.

1. What is the same about all trees?
   - Ⓐ They stay green all year round.
   - Ⓑ They are brown all year round.
   - Ⓒ They have green leaves.

2. Trees that drop their leaves in the fall _____.
   - Ⓐ grow new leaves in the spring
   - Ⓑ grow bigger leaves right away
   - Ⓒ become evergreens

3. How are evergreens different from other trees?
   - Ⓐ Evergreens drop all their leaves at one time, but other trees do not.
   - Ⓑ Evergreens stay green all year round, but other trees do not.
   - Ⓒ Evergreens are always bare, but other trees are not.

RHYMING WORDS

Add one or two letters to make words that rhyme with <u>drop</u>.

1. ____op   2. ____op   3. ____op

Name: _____

Compare and Contrast

WEEK 16 DAY 3

Read the story. Look for ways the brothers are the same and different.

Cody and Jud were ready for spaghetti.
Mom gave each boy a full plate.
Jud twirled spaghetti around his fork.
But he got too much.
It did not fit in his mouth.
The sauce smeared Jud's face.
Cody slurped his spaghetti.
Some spaghetti hit his nose.
Cody's nose was red with sauce.
Then Jud ate some spaghetti with his fingers.
His fingers left red prints on his glass of milk.
Mom took a picture of her red-faced boys.

Fill in the circle next to the correct answer

1. What is the same about the boys?
   Ⓐ They both get messy.
   Ⓑ They both slurp their spaghetti.
   Ⓒ They both eat with their fingers.

2. How is Cody different from Jud?
   Ⓐ Cody eats spaghetti with his fingers, but Jud does not.
   Ⓑ Cody likes spaghetti, but Jud does not.
   Ⓒ Cody slurps spaghetti, but Jud does not.

3. How is Jud different from Cody?
   Ⓐ Jud slurps his spaghetti, but Cody does not.
   Ⓑ Jud's nose is red with sauce, but Cody's is not.
   Ⓒ Jud's glass of milk has red prints, but Cody's does not.

VOWEL SOUNDS

Circle two words in the story that have the vowel sound you hear in <u>mouse</u>.

Name: _____

Compare and Contrast WEEK 16 DAY 4

Read the story. Find out how spiders and insects are the same and different.

Spiders and insects are very small animals.
Their bodies have a hard shell.
But spiders and insects are not the same.
Look at their body parts.
An insect's body has three main parts.
But a spider's body has only two.
Now count the legs.
An insect has six legs.
A spider has eight.
Now look for wings.
Most insects have wings.
Spiders do not fly.

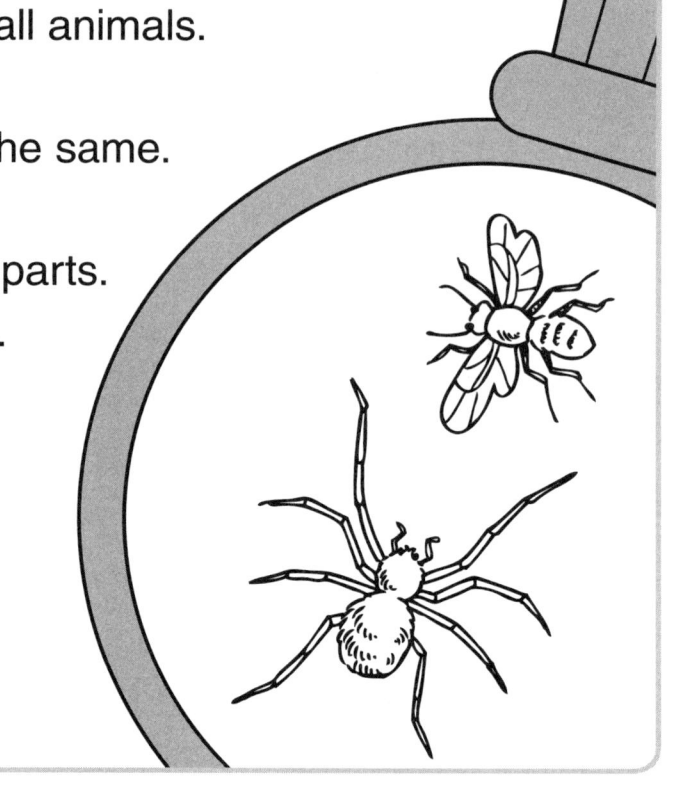

Fill in the circle next to the correct answer.

1. An insect has six legs, and a spider has _____.
   Ⓐ three legs
   Ⓑ six legs
   Ⓒ eight legs

2. Which one tells about spiders and insects?
   Ⓐ They are the same in every way.
   Ⓑ They have hard shells.
   Ⓒ They have eight legs.

3. How is a spider different from an insect?
   Ⓐ A spider has two main body parts, but an insect does not.
   Ⓑ A spider has a hard shell, but an insect does not.
   Ⓒ A spider has wings, but an insect does not.

VOWEL SOUNDS

Circle the sound of y in each word.

1. fl<u>y</u>   ī   ē
2. bod<u>y</u>   ī   ē
3. onl<u>y</u>   ī   ē

104   Daily Reading Comprehension • EMC 3451 • © Evan-Moor Corp.

Name: _____

Compare and Contrast WEEK 16 DAY 5

Read the story. How are a baseball and a basketball the same and different?

A baseball and a basketball are kinds of balls.
They are both used to play sports.
A baseball is white and hard.
Players hit the ball with a bat.
A basketball is orange.
It is filled with air so it can bounce.
Players bounce the ball on a floor.
Both baseballs and basketballs are thrown.
Baseball players use a glove to catch a baseball.
Basketball players catch a basketball with their hands.

Fill in the circle next to the correct answer.

1. Baseballs and basketballs are both _____.
   Ⓐ used in sports
   Ⓑ hit with a bat
   Ⓒ bounced on a floor

2. How is a baseball different from a basketball?
   Ⓐ A baseball is filled with air, but a basketball is not.
   Ⓑ A baseball is white, but a basketball is orange.
   Ⓒ A baseball is bounced on a floor, but a basketball is not.

3. How is a basketball different from a baseball?
   Ⓐ A basketball is thrown, but a baseball is not.
   Ⓑ A basketball is filled with air, but a baseball is not.
   Ⓒ A basketball is a kind of ball, but a baseball is not.

VOWEL SOUNDS

Circle the words that have the vowel sound you hear in <u>and</u>.

1. catch   2. air   3. bat   4. basket   5. ball

© Evan-Moor Corp. • EMC 3451 • Daily Reading Comprehension   105

WEEK 17

Fantasy and Reality

Students determine whether a story or specific information within it are fantastic or realistic.

DAY 1

Say: **This week we will practice telling the difference between what can really happen and what is make-believe. Another word for *make-believe* is *fantasy*. Something that can really happen is called *reality*.** Give an example by telling students something fantastical and something realistic about yourself. (For example: I get to school at 7:30 in the morning. I come in a rocket ship.) Then read the instructions at the top of the page aloud. Ask students to follow along as you read and to decide whether each sentence is real or make-believe. After reading, guide students through the first activity. To be sure they're recognizing the fantasy elements, let students talk about the reasons for their answer choices. Then let students complete the sight words activity with a partner.

DAY 2

Review the skill by making a few statements about weather and asking students to give a thumbs up to what can really happen. (For example: Strong winds knocked branches off a tree. The red and blue raindrops splashed against the window.) Then direct students' attention to the story and read the instructions aloud. Read the story to students as they follow along, reading the words they know. Pause after each sentence, and let students give a thumbs up when the statement is realistic. Then guide students in completing the first activity. For each item, students may first circle the key words. *(can really happen, make-believe, true)* Ask students to read the sight words activity with a partner. Then go over the activity together.

DAY 3

To review the skill, have students play a short game. Volunteers give a statement, and the class decides if it is make-believe or realistic. (You may want to suggest a topic, such as weather or animals.) Then direct students' attention to the story and read the instructions aloud. Read the story, inviting students to follow along and read the words they know. After reading, lead students in completing the first activity. Let them explain the reasons for their answer choices. Instruct students to complete the sight words activity independently. Some students may find it useful to say the letters out loud as they write them.

DAY 4

Ask students to explain the difference between real and make-believe (or use the words *fantasy* and *reality*) to a partner. Then direct students' attention to the illustration, and identify the boy as Cole. Read the instructions aloud. Tell students to follow along as you read the story and to think about each sentence as it is read. After reading, ask for volunteers to read the four sentences in the story that are make-believe. Complete the activities as a class.

DAY 5

Remind students of the skill and tell them that today they will read a story about a grandma and an elf. Ask: **How do you know there will be make-believe things in the story?** (because one of the characters is an elf) Read the instructions aloud. Read the story as students follow along. If needed, read the story a second time before leading students in completing the first activity. Ask students to explain each answer choice. Then have students do the sight words activity in pairs.

Name: _____

Fantasy and Reality

WEEK 17 DAY 1

Read the story. Ask yourself, "What is make-believe and what can happen?"

Hannah ran outside.
It rained every day at 2 o'clock.
She saw clouds form in the sky.
They were mixed with colors.
Some clouds were red and green.
Some were purple and orange.
Then Hannah heard a loud rip!
The clouds ripped open like paper bags.
Hannah held out her hands.
Lollipops fell from the sky.
Hannah liked living in Candy Land!

Fill in the circle next to the correct answer.

1. What in the story can really happen?
   Ⓐ Clouds can form in the sky.
   Ⓑ Clouds can be red and green.
   Ⓒ Clouds can rip open like bags.

2. What in the story is make-believe?
   Ⓐ A girl watches clouds.
   Ⓑ A girl runs outside.
   Ⓒ Rain falls at 2 o'clock every day.

3. What in the story is make-believe?
   Ⓐ Candy falls from the sky.
   Ⓑ Candy comes in colors.
   Ⓒ Lollipops are candy.

SIGHT WORDS

Circle the two words that are the same.

1. white   2. with   3. will   4. with   5. when

Name: _____

Fantasy and Reality

WEEK 17 DAY 2

Read the story. Ask yourself, "What is make-believe and what can happen?"

A zoo is a busy place.
Polar bears slide into the water.
Unicorns run in the grass.
Penguins flap their flippers.
Seals eat tasty fish.
Owls hoot high in the trees.
Elephants shake their trunks.
Snakes wiggle up branches.
Tigers sell bags of popcorn.
Zebras chat on their phones.
And monkeys swing from the trees.

Fill in the circle next to the correct answer.

1. What in the story can really happen?
   Ⓐ Zebras can talk on phones.
   Ⓑ Tigers can sell popcorn.
   Ⓒ An owl can sit in a tree.

2. What in the story is make-believe?
   Ⓐ seals eating fish
   Ⓑ unicorns in the grass
   Ⓒ snakes wiggling

3. Which one is true?
   Ⓐ Zebras have phones.
   Ⓑ Tigers sell things.
   Ⓒ Monkeys swing from trees.

SIGHT WORDS

Circle the word that correctly completes the sentence.

Do you want a glass (off   of) apple juice?

Name: _____

Fantasy and Reality

WEEK 17 DAY 3

Read the story. Ask yourself, "What is make-believe and what can happen?"

Ann was helping her mom make a cake.
Ann poured flour and sugar into a bowl.
Then Ann's mom added the eggs.
She was ready to mix.
Ann's mom could not find the spoon.
Ann looked hard at the stove.
She could see right through it.
She saw a spoon under the stove.
Ann said, "Just a minute."
Ann lifted the stove off the floor.
"There's the spoon, Mom," said Ann.
"Thanks, dear," said Ann's mom.

Fill in the circle next to the correct answer.

1. What in the story can really happen?
   Ⓐ A girl can help her mom make a cake.
   Ⓑ A girl can lift a stove.
   Ⓒ A girl can see through a stove.

2. What in the story is make-believe?
   Ⓐ A mom says thanks.
   Ⓑ A girl has superpowers.
   Ⓒ A spoon slips under a stove.

3. What does Ann do to find the spoon?
   Ⓐ Ann looks under the stove.
   Ⓑ Ann pulls the stove away from the wall.
   Ⓒ Ann looks through the stove.

SIGHT WORDS

Write the letters on the lines to spell the word just.

1. ___ ust   2. j ___ t   3. j ___ s ___

Name: _____

Fantasy and Reality

WEEK 17 DAY 4

Read the story. Ask yourself, "What is make-believe and what can happen?"

Cole put on his pajamas.
He wore the same pajamas every night.
He looked like a race car driver.
Then Cole jumped into his race car bed.
Oops! He had forgotten to brush his teeth.
Cole grabbed the steering wheel on his bed.
"Vroom! Vroom!" yelled Cole.
The bed zoomed out of Cole's bedroom.
It raced down the hallway.
Then the bed stopped with a screech.
Cole went into the bathroom.
The bed beeped its horn so Cole would hurry.

Fill in the circle next to the correct answer.

1. What in the story can really happen?
   Ⓐ A bed can move like a car.
   Ⓑ A boy can put on his pajamas.
   Ⓒ A bed can obey a boy.

2. What in the story is make-believe?
   Ⓐ A boy wears pajamas to bed.
   Ⓑ A boy drives his bed like a car.
   Ⓒ A boy goes to brush his teeth.

3. Why does Cole race his bed?
   Ⓐ He needs a glass of water.
   Ⓑ He needs to get his pajamas.
   Ⓒ He needs to brush his teeth.

SIGHT WORDS

Circle the word that correctly completes the sentence.

Cole looks (live   like) a race car driver.

Name: _____

WEEK 17
Fantasy and Reality **DAY 5**

Read the story. Ask yourself, "What is make-believe and what can happen?"

Grandma looked at the seeds.
An elf had given them to her.
He said to plant the seeds by a wall.
So Grandma did as the elf said.
She wondered what would grow.
The next day, Grandma had a surprise.
Branches covered all the walls of her house.
All kinds of fruit hung from every branch.
Apples mixed with pears.
Plums hung with peaches.
Oranges were in between.
Grandma told her friends to pick some fruit.

Fill in the circle next to the correct answer.

1. What in the story can really happen?
   Ⓐ A grandma can talk to an elf.
   Ⓑ Fruit can grow from seeds.
   Ⓒ An elf can have seeds.

2. What in the story is make-believe?
   Ⓐ Seeds can grow in one day.
   Ⓑ A grandma plants seeds.
   Ⓒ Apples grow on branches.

3. What is true about fruit?
   Ⓐ Fruit seeds can be planted in the ground.
   Ⓑ All kinds of fruit grow on the same branch.
   Ⓒ Fruit grows from magic seeds.

SIGHT WORDS

Circle the word that correctly completes the sentence.

Mom reads Louis a story (very   every) night.

© Evan-Moor Corp. • EMC 3451 • Daily Reading Comprehension

WEEK 18

Prediction

With Prediction, students use clues from a story and prior knowledge to predict what will happen next. Students understand that good predictions follow logically from the events of the story.

DAY 1

Tell students that this week they will practice the reading skill called *Prediction*. Say: **To predict means to make a good guess about what may happen next. Good readers pay attention to what characters say and do. They use these clues to predict what will probably happen next.** Direct students' attention to the story, and read the instructions at the top of the page aloud. Read the story aloud as students follow along. Then lead them in completing the first activity. For items 1 and 2, let students tell the story clues that can help them make predictions. Complete the word meanings activity together, and then ask students to stand and jiggle.

DAY 2

Review the skill by recalling the prediction made about Dad and Sparky in the Day 1 story. (Dad will take Sparky for a walk.) Ask students to recall Dad's actions that were clues to making the prediction. (Dad gets Sparky's leash; Dad whistles for Sparky, etc.) Say: **Today we will make predictions about a baby bird.** Read the instructions at the top of the page aloud to focus students on the task. Instruct students to repeat each sentence after you, touching each word as they say it. Pause when necessary to explain vocabulary, such as *down* and *rim*. After reading, lead students through the first activity. Have them relate story clues that helped them make the prediction. Then direct attention to the word meanings activity. Instruct students to point to the labeled areas of the bird and read the labels with you. Have them complete the activity and check their responses.

DAY 3

Remind students that what characters say and do are clues to predict what will probably happen next. Say: **Today we will read about Liam and his jacket. Pay close attention to what Liam does.** Read the instructions, and then read the story aloud. After reading, guide students in completing the first activity. For each answer choice in item 1, ask: **Does the story give clues that this will happen? If so, what are the clues?** For item 3, ask students to explain their answer choices. Then do the word meanings activity together. Say: **It's good to look back at the story for clues about what a word means.** Help students locate the word *store* in the story and read it in context. After circling their answer, ask students to tell a partner two things they would store in a big pocket.

DAY 4

Remind students of the skill. Then say that today's story is about a girl named Ava and her mom. Read the instructions aloud. Read the story as students follow along. After reading the sentence about buying peanut butter, ask students where the story takes place. (grocery store, supermarket) After completing the story, help students do the first activity. For items 1 and 2, ask students to tell what Ava and her mom did that are clues for making the predictions. Then complete the word meanings activity. Recall that Ava and her mom bought a loaf of bread. Ask students to circle the loaf of bread. Ask students to explain the difference between a loaf of bread and a slice of bread.

DAY 5

Read the instructions at the top of the page aloud. Then tell students that today's story is about a boy named Seth. Say: **Pay attention to what Seth does. His actions are clues for predicting what will happen next.** Read the story aloud as students follow along, reading the words they know. Complete the first activity together. When doing the word meanings activity, read the word *rumble* in context, and then guide students in choosing the two correct answers.

Name: _____

Prediction — WEEK 18, DAY 1

Read the story. Ask yourself, "What will probably happen next?"

Dad pats his pocket.
He makes sure his house keys are there.
Then he opens the kitchen drawer.
He pulls out Sparky's leash.
Dad jiggles the leash and whistles.
Sparky wakes up from her nap.
She knows what that whistle means.
She likes the sound of the jiggling leash.
Sparky hurries over to Dad, wagging her tail.
Dad hooks the leash to Sparky's collar.

Fill in the circle next to the correct answer.

1. What will probably happen next?
    Ⓐ Dad will take Sparky for a walk.
    Ⓑ Dad will throw a ball for Sparky to chase.
    Ⓒ Dad will feed dinner to Sparky.

2. What will Sparky probably do after Dad puts on her leash?
    Ⓐ She will go to the door.
    Ⓑ She will lie down and sleep.
    Ⓒ She will bite Dad.

3. How does Dad show Sparky that it is time for a walk?
    Ⓐ He looks for his house keys.
    Ⓑ He says, "Let's go for a walk!"
    Ⓒ He jiggles the leash and whistles.

WORD MEANINGS

Circle another way to say that Dad jiggles Sparky's leash.

1. Dad shakes Sparky's leash.
2. Dad throws Sparky's leash.

Name: _____

Prediction WEEK 18 DAY 2

Read the story. Ask yourself, "What will probably happen next?"

Crack went the eggs.
The baby birds were hatched.
They opened their beaks wide.
They were hungry for some bugs.
Soft gray down covered their bodies.
Days later, the down fell out.
The baby birds grew feathers.
They needed feathers to fly.
More days passed, and the babies got bigger.
They hardly fit in their nest.
And they were hungry for more food.
Finally, one baby stood on the rim of the nest.
It flapped its wings hard.

Fill in the circle next to the correct answer.

1. What will probably happen next?
   Ⓐ The baby bird will try to walk.
   Ⓑ The baby bird will try to fly.
   Ⓒ The baby bird will grow feathers.

2. Which of these shows that one baby is ready to leave the nest?
   Ⓐ It stands on the rim of the nest.
   Ⓑ It has gray down.
   Ⓒ It can open its beak wide.

3. Which one is true about baby birds?
   Ⓐ They make their own nests.
   Ⓑ They need feathers before they can fly.
   Ⓒ They fly right after they are born.

WORD MEANINGS

Circle the arrow that points to the <u>down</u> on the baby bird.

Name: _____ Prediction **WEEK 18 DAY 3**

Read the story. Ask yourself, "What will probably happen next?"

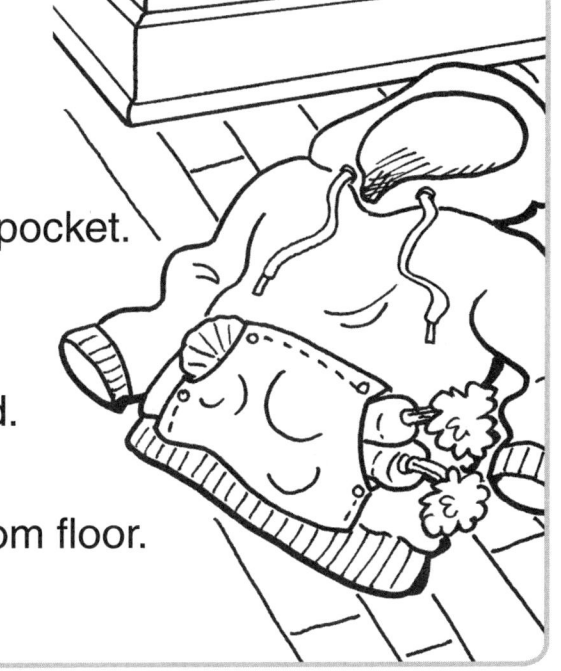

Liam's jacket has a great big pocket.
The pocket stretches across the front.
It's easy for Liam to reach inside.
He can store a lot of things in that big pocket.
Last week, Liam put in a few carrots.
He stuck in some seashells, too.
He added the dead bugs he had found.
And he put in a soft peach.
Then Liam left his jacket on his bedroom floor.
He forgot about it for a few days.

Fill in the circle next to the correct answer.

1. What will probably happen next?
   Ⓐ The jacket will be smaller.
   Ⓑ The jacket will be ready to wear.
   Ⓒ The jacket will smell.

2. Which word describes the pocket?
   Ⓐ clean
   Ⓑ handy
   Ⓒ small

3. What will Liam probably do from now on?
   Ⓐ He will empty the pocket every day.
   Ⓑ He will stop eating peaches.
   Ⓒ He will put dead bugs in the pocket.

WORD MEANINGS

What does the word <u>store</u> mean in the story?
Circle your answer.

   1. a place to buy things   2. to save

© Evan-Moor Corp. • EMC 3451 • Daily Reading Comprehension

Name: _____

Prediction WEEK 18 DAY 4

Read the story. Ask yourself, "What will probably happen next?"

The doors to the store slid open.
Ava's mom carried a shopping bag.
She and Ava did not need a shopping cart.
They were going to buy just a few things.
Ava's mom got a jar of smooth peanut butter.
Ava chose some grape jelly.
They picked out a loaf of bread together.
The bread was already sliced.
Ava placed a carton of milk at the bottom of the bag.
Then Ava and her mom were ready to pay.
It was lunchtime, and they were hungry.

Fill in the circle next to the correct answer.

1. What will Ava and her mom probably do next?
   Ⓐ They will buy many more things.
   Ⓑ They will go to a movie.
   Ⓒ They will make lunch for themselves.

2. What will Ava and her mom probably make for lunch?
   Ⓐ cheese sandwiches
   Ⓑ chicken soup
   Ⓒ peanut butter and jelly sandwiches

3. Why did Ava and her mom use a shopping bag?
   Ⓐ They were buying just a few things.
   Ⓑ The shopping carts were gone.
   Ⓒ Ava was too big to sit in a cart.

WORD MEANINGS

Circle the <u>loaf</u> of bread.

1.    2.

Name: _____

Prediction WEEK 18 DAY 5

Read the story. Ask yourself, "What will probably happen next?"

The kids at school called Seth "Speedy."
Seth did everything fast.
One day, Seth stayed still.
He sat on a bench during recess.
And he gave his snack to a friend.
Seth seemed sleepy.
His nose dripped like a leaky pipe.
And he coughed with a rumble.
Seth's teacher put her hand on his forehead.
Seth felt hot.
She sent him to the school office.
Seth just sat until his dad came to get him.

Fill in the circle next to the correct answer.

1. What will Seth probably do next?
   Ⓐ Seth will play in his yard.
   Ⓑ Seth will go to bed.
   Ⓒ Seth will clean his room.

2. What will Seth probably do when he feels better?
   Ⓐ run to school
   Ⓑ sleep during recess
   Ⓒ cough and sneeze

3. Which sentence from the story tells that Seth was sick?
   Ⓐ "Seth did everything fast."
   Ⓑ "The kids at school called Seth 'Speedy.'"
   Ⓒ "Seth felt hot."

WORD MEANINGS

Circle all the things that can make a <u>rumble</u>.

1. a big truck   2. a kitten   3. a small bird   4. thunder

WEEK 19

Main Idea and Details

Students read to understand the central message of a passage or story. They also monitor their comprehension of important details.

DAY 1

Tell students that this week they will practice the reading skill *Main Idea and Details*. Say: **Every story has a main idea, which is what the story is mostly about. Knowing the main idea helps you understand what you are reading. Stories also have details that tell more about the main idea.** Read the instructions at the top of the page aloud. Ask: **Does a poem have a main idea?** (Yes. A poem is about something.) Read the poem aloud as students follow along. Reread the poem and point out that each stanza tells about the plants goats eat. Then guide students in doing the first activity. For item 2, let students explain why A and C are incorrect. (The poem says, "No meat will do.") Complete the phonics activity together.

DAY 2

Tell students that today they will read a story about a girl named Ali. Read the instructions aloud, and then say: **What the story is *mostly* about is called the *Main Idea*. Pay attention to what most of the sentences say about Ali.** Read the story aloud as students follow along, reading the words they know. After reading, lead students in completing the first activity. Ask questions that encourage students to think through their answer choices. (For example: Is Ali in the library? How do you know she's not?) Point out that item 1 asks about the main idea of the story. Items 2 and 3 ask about story details. Next, have students complete the phonics activity with a partner and then check their answers together.

DAY 3

Review the skill by asking a few questions which students answer by nodding their heads for *yes* or shaking them for *no*. Ask: **Is what a story is about the main idea of the story?** (yes) **Is the main idea the same as a detail?** (no) **Does every story have a main idea?** (yes) **Does every poem have a main idea?** (yes) Tell students that today they will read a story about a first-grader named Chad. Read the instructions aloud to focus students on the purpose for reading. Read the story twice as students follow along. After reading, guide students in completing the first activity. For item 1, help them see why B is incorrect. Complete the phonics activity together. Read each word, accentuating the *g*. Have students repeat the word after you. Pause for students to circle their answer choices. Then check their responses together.

DAY 4

Ask students to explain *Main Idea* to a partner. (what a story is mostly about) Then direct their attention to today's story, and read the instructions aloud. Then read the story aloud as students follow along. Write *Caves* in a box on the board. Read the story again, stopping often to ask students what details they heard about caves. Use the facts to create a simple web with *Caves* at the center. Keep the details short and simple. (bugs and spiders deep inside, dark and cool, etc.) Then guide students in completing the first activity. After item 1 is answered, replace *Caves* with *Some Facts About Caves* as the title of the web. Lead students in finding details that support the correct choices for items 2 and 3. Complete the phonics activity together. Read each sentence slowly, allowing students time to circle their responses.

DAY 5

Tell students that today they will read a story about Crab and Hare. Say: **Stories have a main idea. The main idea is what the *whole* story is *mostly* about. Does the picture give you any clues to what the story is about?** Read the instructions and story aloud as students follow along. Lead students in completing the first activity. Have them refer to story details to help determine the correct answers. Then do the phonics activity together.

Main Idea and Details — WEEK 19 DAY 1

Read the poem. Ask yourself, "What is this poem about?"

Goats are plant eaters,
No meat will do.
They want hay to crunch
And bushes to chew.

They think trees and bark
Are really quite yummy.
And roses and weeds
Are good for their tummy.

If you need some mowing,
I give you this clue.
A small herd of goats
Will do the mowing for you.

Fill in the circle next to the correct answer.

1. What does the poem say about goats?
   Ⓐ They make good pets.
   Ⓑ They eat all day long.
   Ⓒ They eat all kinds of plants.

2. Goats like to eat _____.
   Ⓐ bugs
   Ⓑ flowers
   Ⓒ mice

3. Which word means "a group of goats"?
   Ⓐ crunch
   Ⓑ bark
   Ⓒ herd

VOWEL SOUNDS

Circle the two letters in each word that spell the long o sound.

goat   mow   toe   slow

Name: _____

Main Idea and Details WEEK 19 DAY 2

Read the story. Ask yourself, "What is this story about?"

Ali sat with a big book in her lap.
She liked that book best of all.
Her mother had made the book.
The book was all about Ali.
Ali slowly turned each page.
There was a picture of Ali when she was born.
She wore a pink bow taped to her bald head.
Ali thought she looked cute!
Another picture showed Ali learning to walk.
Ali read that **cookie** was her first word.
She wished she could remember being a baby.

Fill in the circle next to the correct answer.

1. What is the story about?
   Ⓐ A girl goes to the library.
   Ⓑ A girl looks at her baby book.
   Ⓒ A girl reads a story.

2. What is something you learn about Ali?
   Ⓐ Ali likes to make books about herself.
   Ⓑ Ali likes to take pictures.
   Ⓒ Ali wonders about being a baby.

3. Which one tells about Ali when she was a baby?
   Ⓐ Ali was bald.
   Ⓑ Ali's first word was "bye-bye."
   Ⓒ Ali wore a pink hat.

VOWEL SOUNDS

Circle the word in each pair that has a long vowel sound.

1. tap   tape   2. mad   made   3. cute   cut   4. plane   plan

Name: _____

Main Idea and Details

WEEK 19 DAY 3

Read the story. Ask yourself, "What is this story about?"

The first-graders wrote stories.
Chad's teacher is passing them back.
Chad crosses his fingers.
He hopes to see a star on his paper.
His teacher puts blue stars on the best stories.
Then she hangs the star stories in the hallway.
Chad worked hard on his story.
He created a make-believe animal.
The animal has the legs of a giraffe.
It has the body of a zebra.
Its nose is the trunk of an elephant.
And best of all, it roars like a lion.

Fill in the circle next to the correct answer.

1. What is the story about?
   Ⓐ A boy wants his story to get a star.
   Ⓑ An animal has mixed-up parts.
   Ⓒ A teacher passes out stories.

2. Chad's animal _____.
   Ⓐ has eight legs
   Ⓑ is a lion
   Ⓒ is not real

3. What does Chad's teacher do with the star stories?
   Ⓐ She puts a gold star on them.
   Ⓑ She hangs them up.
   Ⓒ She shows them to the principal.

CONSONANT SOUNDS

Circle the sound of g that you hear in each word.

1. le<u>g</u>   g   j
2. <u>g</u>iraffe   g   j
3. fin<u>g</u>er   g   j

Name: _____

Main Idea and Details

WEEK 19 DAY 4

Read the story. Ask yourself, "What is this story about?"

Caves are large holes in the ground.
They are dark and cool on the inside.
Some caves have rocks that hang
   from the ceiling.
Creatures live in caves.
Some of the animals come and go.
Bears sleep in caves during the winter.
Bats hang in caves to rest.
Some of the animals never leave their caves.
Bugs and spiders live deep inside.
The cave is their home.
They are always in the dark.

Fill in the circle next to the correct answer.

1. What is the story about?
   Ⓐ rocks found in caves
   Ⓑ how to explore caves
   Ⓒ some facts about caves

2. Which one tells about animals that live deep inside caves?
   Ⓐ They come and they go.
   Ⓑ They live in the dark.
   Ⓒ They hang from the ceiling.

3. Which one is a fact about caves?
   Ⓐ Caves give animals a place to rest.
   Ⓑ Caves are full of sun.
   Ⓒ Caves are hot on the inside.

VOWEL SOUNDS

Circle five words in the story that have the same vowel sound as <u>treat</u>.

Name: _____

Main Idea and Details

WEEK 19 DAY 5

Read the story. Ask yourself, "What is this story about?"

Crab and Hare grow carrots together.
But Hare wants to eat them all.
Crab has a plan. He says,
"Hare, I dare you to race me to the carrot pile!
The first one there wins all of the carrots."
Hare takes the dare and begins to run.
He does not feel Crab grab onto his tail.
Soon, Hare is one step away from the pile.
Crab lets go of Hare's tail.
Crab sails through the air.
He lands right on top of the carrots.
"I win!" yells Crab.
All Hare does is stare.

Fill in the circle next to the correct answer.

1. What is the story about?
   Ⓐ a pile of carrots
   Ⓑ a hare's tail
   Ⓒ a crab that tricks a hare

2. Which one tells about Crab?
   Ⓐ Crab will not share.
   Ⓑ Crab runs fast.
   Ⓒ Crab is smart.

3. How does the story end?
   Ⓐ Hare tricks Crab.
   Ⓑ Crab wins the pile of carrots.
   Ⓒ Crab and Hare eat the carrots.

RHYMING WORDS

Circle the words in the story that rhyme with <u>hare</u>.

WEEK 20

Who, What, and Where

Students read to determine "who" (the main character), "what" (the main character's actions), and "where" (the setting).

DAY 1

Write *Who*, *What*, and *Where* on the board. Point to each word as you tell students they will practice finding *Who* the main characters of a story are, *What* the characters do, and *Where* the story takes place. Then read the instructions at the top of the page aloud. Say: **The beginning of a story or poem usually tells *who* the story or poem is about. Read the first verse of the poem with me to find out *who* the poem is about.** After reading the first verse, ask students to circle the two words that tell *who* the poem is about. (fruit pickers) Then ask: **Did you find out *where* the story takes place?** (yes, at an apple farm) **Let's read the rest of the poem to find out *what* the fruit pickers do at the apple farm.** Read the remaining verses aloud together. Then guide students to complete the first activity, referring to the poem for answers. Have students complete the sight words activity with a partner.

DAY 2

Review the skill by writing *Who*, *What*, and *Where* on the board. Tell students that you are going to give them some clues and they are to answer with one of the words on the board. Then say: **The place a story happens** (where), **The characters in the story** (who), **The things the characters do** (what). Remind students that the main characters of a story may be animals. Read the instructions and the story as students follow along or read with you. Stop after the second sentence and ask: **Who are the characters in this story?** (ants) Read the third sentence and ask: **What do you think the rest of the sentences will tell us?** (what jobs the ants do) While reading, help students notice the three kinds of ants mentioned and the job each does. Complete the activities together.

DAY 3

Direct students' attention to the illustration, and recall that a picture often tells the main character of a story. Read the instructions aloud. Then read the first sentence aloud. Ask students to raise their hands if they think the story is about a camel and how it lives in a desert. Read the story as students follow along or read with you. After reading, ask them if most of the story tells how a camel can live in a desert. (yes) Then write *Who*, *What*, and *Where* on the board and have students review the story information. Summarize the story in one sentence, such as: A camel's body is made to live in a desert. Help students complete the first activity, using details from the story to support their choices. Instruct students to do the sight words activity independently. Some may find it useful to say the letters out loud as they write.

DAY 4

Write *Who*, *What*, and *Where* on the board. Have students tell a partner what those words mean when reading a story. (the characters, the characters' actions, the place the story happens) Then direct students' attention to the illustration. Say: **Look at the picture. Who is this story probably about?** (two boys and a woman) **Let's read to find out who they are, what they are doing, and where they are.** Read the story aloud as students follow along or read with you. Lead them in completing the first activity. For items 1 and 2, help them understand why some choices are correct and others are not. Complete the sight words activity together.

DAY 5

Direct students' attention to the illustration. Ask: **Does this picture show *who* the story is about?** (no) Read the instructions aloud. Then read the story as students follow along or read with you. After reading, guide students in completing the activities.

Name: _____

Who, What, and Where — WEEK 20 DAY 1

Read the poem. Ask yourself, "Who? What? Where?"

Out at the apple farm
It is harvest time.
Up the tall ladders
The fruit pickers climb.

On the green branches
That swing overhead,
Apples are hanging
All rosy and red.

The apples are ripe,
All juicy and sweet.
The pickers fill baskets
Of good apples to eat.

Fill in the circle next to the correct answer.

1. Who is talked about in the poem?
   Ⓐ people who grow apples
   Ⓑ people who pick apples
   Ⓒ people who eat apples

2. What do the fruit pickers do?
   Ⓐ swing overhead
   Ⓑ eat the apples
   Ⓒ fill up baskets

3. Where does the poem take place?
   Ⓐ on top of an apple tree
   Ⓑ in a supermarket
   Ⓒ on an apple farm

SIGHT WORDS

Circle the two words that are the same.

1. out   2. our   3. one   4. old   5. out

Name: _____

Who, What, and Where

WEEK 20 DAY 2

Read the story. Ask yourself, "Who? What? Where?"

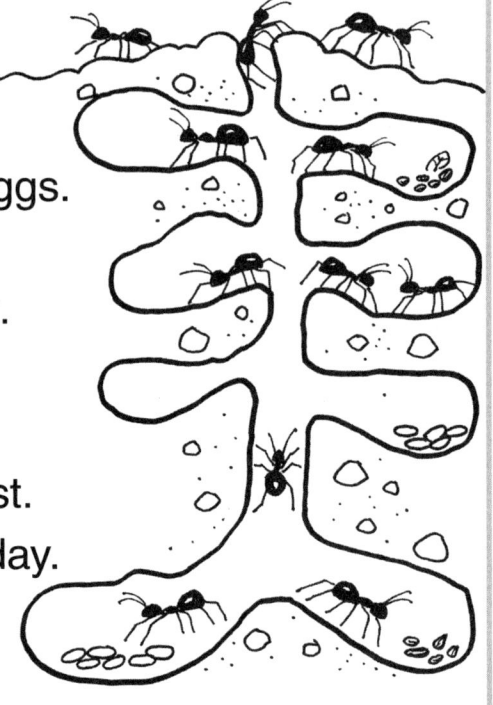

Ants live under the ground.
Ant homes are called nests.
Every ant in the nest has a job to do.
One ant is the queen that lays all of the eggs.
A few ants are guards.
They watch for danger outside of the nest.
Most ants are worker ants.
Some worker ants care for the baby ants.
Some workers dig more rooms for the nest.
A lot of worker ants leave the nest every day.
They search for food.
And they share what they find.

Fill in the circle next to the correct answer.

1. The story is mostly about _____.
   Ⓐ ants and the jobs they do
   Ⓑ ants that look for food
   Ⓒ ants that lay eggs

2. What is a job of some worker ants?
   Ⓐ They lay eggs.
   Ⓑ They look for danger.
   Ⓒ They care for baby ants.

3. Where do ants live?
   Ⓐ in nests in trees
   Ⓑ in nests under the ground
   Ⓒ in nests on top of the ground

SIGHT WORDS

Circle the two words that are the same.

1. our   2. out   3. one   4. on   5. one

Name: _____

Who, What, and Where

WEEK 20 DAY 3

Read the story. Ask yourself, "Who? What? Where?"

A camel's body helps it live in a desert.
A desert is hot and dry.
There is not much food or water.
A camel has a hump on its back.
The hump holds fat.
A camel's body feeds off that fat for a long time.

Sand blows and swirls in a desert.
A camel has two rows of long eyelashes.
They help keep the sand out of its eyes.
A camel closes its nose when the sand blows.
The feet of a camel are big and strong.
They do not sink in the sand.

Fill in the circle next to the correct answer.

1. Where do camels live?
   Ⓐ in cold and icy lands
   Ⓑ in rainy forests
   Ⓒ in hot and dry deserts

2. The story is mostly about _____.
   Ⓐ the way camels walk in sand
   Ⓑ how camels can live in deserts
   Ⓒ the way sand blows in deserts

3. What keeps the sand out of a camel's eyes?
   Ⓐ a lot of eyelashes
   Ⓑ a lot of fur on its head
   Ⓒ eyes that open and close

SIGHT WORDS

Write the letters on the lines to spell the word <u>there</u>.

1. t___ ___ ___ ___   2. ___ ___ere   3. th___ ___e

Name: _____

Who, What, and Where WEEK 20 DAY 4

Read the story. Ask yourself, "Who? What? Where?"

Hector and José hurried into Fun Land.
They loved the fast and scary rides!
Aunt Maria let the boys choose the rides.
They started with the bumper cars.
Aunt Maria's body shook with each bump.
Then her stomach twirled on the flying rockets.
Her hair flew as the roller coaster zoomed.
And she got splashed on the water ride.
Finally, Aunt Maria said, "It's my turn to pick.
  I pick the train ride."
"But that's the slowest ride here!" whined Hector.
"I know," said Aunt Maria with a smile.

Fill in the circle next to the correct answer.

1. What is the story mostly about?
   Ⓐ getting wet on a water ride
   Ⓑ making rules for Fun Land
   Ⓒ having fun at Fun Land

2. Who is the story mostly about?
   Ⓐ Hector
   Ⓑ José and Hector
   Ⓒ Aunt Maria

3. Where does the story take place?
   Ⓐ at a park with rides
   Ⓑ at a farm
   Ⓒ at a circus

SIGHT WORDS

Circle the word that correctly completes the sentence.

"I (now   know) the answer," said José.

Name: _____

Who, What, and Where

WEEK 20 DAY 5

Read the story. Ask yourself, "Who? What? Where?"

Remy yawned as she got in the car.
Dad drove to the top of a hill.
They were far from the lights of the city.
The sky was black except for twinkling stars.
Dad and Remy sat on the hood of the car.
They stared at the night sky.
"I see one!" cried Remy.
She pointed to a shooting star.
The star whooshed across the sky.
Then the star faded away.
Whoosh! Whoosh!
More shooting stars flashed by.
Remy was not sleepy anymore.

Fill in the circle next to the correct answer.

1. Who is the story about?
   Ⓐ Remy and her dad
   Ⓑ Remy and her brother
   Ⓒ Remy and her mom

2. What are the characters doing?
   Ⓐ watching shooting stars
   Ⓑ looking at the sun set
   Ⓒ counting stars in the sky

3. Where does the story take place?
   Ⓐ in a city full of lights
   Ⓑ on a hilltop
   Ⓒ in a backyard

SIGHT WORDS

Circle the word that correctly completes the sentence.

Jake will run (form   from) his house to the park.

WEEK 21

Sequence

Students practice Sequence to determine the order of events or steps in a process.

DAY 1

Tell students that this week they will practice the reading skill called *Sequence*. Say: **Sequence is the order in which you do something.** Read the instructions at the top of the page aloud. Then say: **Today's story has signal words that tell the order in which you make a sun print. Often the signal words are at the beginning of sentences.** Ask students to find the first signal word in the story and circle it. *(First)* Let them call out the remaining signal words to circle. *(Next, Then, After that, After an hour)* Then read the story as students follow along or read with you. After reading, complete the first activity with students. Have them circle the signal word(s) in an item before attempting to answer it. *(last, Right after, Before)* Allow a short time for students to complete the word meanings activity independently.

DAY 2

Say: *Sequence* **is the order in which things happen. Today we will read about a girl named Tori and the order in which she makes a breakfast pizza. Picture the breakfast pizza in your mind. That can help you remember Tori's steps for making it.** Read the instructions aloud, and then read the story as students follow along or read with you. After reading, ask students to recall the four steps Tori takes to make the pizza. Let students act out each step as it is said. (spreads cream cheese, puts on apple slices, adds yellow cheese, puts on nuts) Then lead students in completing the first activity. Write the words *triangle* and *circle* on the board. Then instruct students to do the word meanings activity independently.

DAY 3

Review *Sequence* as the order in which things happen. Mention that today's story tells about six animals trying to pull a huge carrot out of the ground. Read the instructions aloud. Ask: **What can we do to help remember the order in which the animals pull?** Read the story. As you read, use the suggested technique for remembering the order of the animals. (For example: Draw a carrot on the board. Behind the carrot, write each animal's name, one behind the other, as it appears in the story.) Then guide students through the first activity. Refer to the suggested aide for help. Instruct students to do the word meanings activity with a partner.

DAY 4

Review the reading skill. Tell students that today's story is about ants called leafcutters. Say: **You probably do not know about leafcutter ants. Good readers picture what they are reading in their minds to help them understand new information.** Read the instructions aloud. Remind students to picture the story. Read the story as students follow along or read with you. Ask students to share some things they pictured. Then lead them in doing the first activity, beginning with circling key words. *(After, Before, first)* Complete the word meanings activity. Have students find and read the word *jaw* in the story in context and circle their answers.

DAY 5

Say: **You know about how signal words help us to understand the sequence of a story. Today we will read a story that tells** *when* **things happen. Let's look through the story and find the signal words that tell** *when***.** *(Last summer, This summer, Next summer)* Read the instructions aloud, and then read the story as students follow along. Use the signal words to understand the sequence of events. Guide students in completing the first activity. Then do the word meanings activity. Help students look back at the story for clues about the meaning of the word *pier*.

Name: _____

WEEK 21
Sequence **DAY 1**

Read the directions. Ask yourself, "What are the steps in making a sun print?"

I like to make sun prints.
First, I get a sheet of dark paper.
Next, I pick some leaves.
Then, I put the paper on the ground.
I spread the leaves all over the paper.
After that, I set a small rock on each leaf.
The leaves then will not blow away.
The paper stays in the hot sun.
After an hour, I take off the rocks and leaves.
I can see the shapes of the leaves.
The sun has made a print for me.

Fill in the circle next to the correct answer.

1. The last thing I do to make a sun print is to _____.
   Ⓐ set a rock on each leaf
   Ⓑ take off the rocks and leaves
   Ⓒ place the paper in the sun

2. Right after I spread the leaves on the paper, I _____.
   Ⓐ set a rock on each leaf
   Ⓑ leave the paper in the hot sun
   Ⓒ pick some flowers

3. Before I set the leaves on the paper, I _____.
   Ⓐ put the paper on the ground
   Ⓑ set a rock on each leaf
   Ⓒ leave the paper in the hot sun

WORD MEANINGS

Circle the word that correctly completes the sentence.

I will (sit   set) the dish on the table.

© Evan-Moor Corp. • EMC 3451 • Daily Reading Comprehension

Name: _____

Sequence WEEK 21 DAY 2

Read the story. Ask yourself, "What are the steps for making a breakfast pizza?"

Tori likes to eat pizza for breakfast.
She likes to make the pizza, too.
Tori starts with the bottom half of a bagel.
She spreads the bagel with cream cheese.
Then, Tori's mom cuts an apple into slices.
Tori puts the apple slices on the cream cheese.
Next, she adds some yellow cheese.
Finally, she puts a few nuts on the top.
Mom puts the pizza in a hot oven.
Tori gets dressed while the pizza bakes.
The cheese is bubbly by the time she's ready.

Fill in the circle next to the correct answer.

1. What does Tori put on the bagel first?
   Ⓐ cream cheese
   Ⓑ yellow cheese
   Ⓒ butter

2. What goes on the pizza right after the apples?
   Ⓐ yellow cheese
   Ⓑ the top half of the bagel
   Ⓒ nuts

3. What is the last thing Tori puts on the bagel?
   Ⓐ yellow cheese
   Ⓑ nuts
   Ⓒ apples

WORD MEANINGS

Write the name of the shape that is on the bottom.

Name: _____

Sequence

WEEK 21 DAY 3

Read the story. Ask yourself, "In what order did the animals pull?"

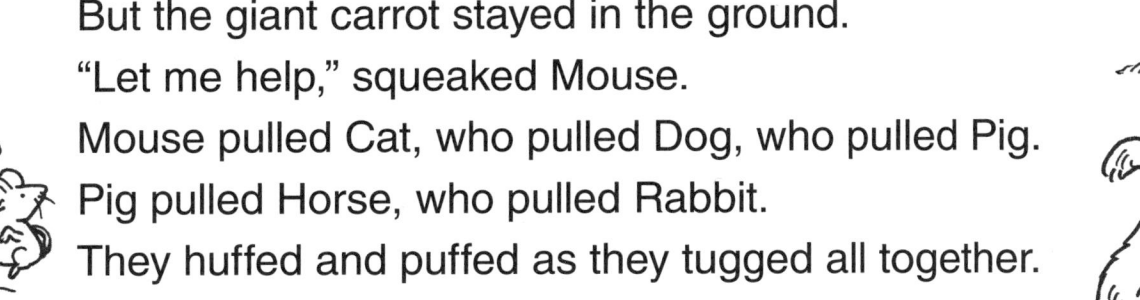

The carrot top was as tall as a bush.
Rabbit pulled and tugged.
But the carrot would not come out.
Horse offered to help, and then so did Pig.
Dog came along and held on to Pig.
Cat put her paws around Dog.
The animals tugged until they all fell down.
But the giant carrot stayed in the ground.
"Let me help," squeaked Mouse.
Mouse pulled Cat, who pulled Dog, who pulled Pig.
Pig pulled Horse, who pulled Rabbit.
They huffed and puffed as they tugged all together.
Ha! Out came the carrot.

Fill in the circle next to the correct answer.

1. Who was the last animal to try to pull out the carrot?
   Ⓐ Rabbit
   Ⓑ Mouse
   Ⓒ Horse

2. Who held on to Pig?
   Ⓐ Horse
   Ⓑ Mouse
   Ⓒ Dog

3. Who was the fifth animal to try to tug out the carrot?
   Ⓐ Horse
   Ⓑ Dog
   Ⓒ Cat

WORD MEANINGS

Circle the word in the story that means about the same as <u>pulled</u>.

Name: _____

Sequence **WEEK 21 DAY 4**

Read the story. Ask yourself, "How do the ants grow their food?"

Leafcutter ants are farmers.
They use leaves to grow their food.
First, the ants climb onto the leaves.
Next, each ant cuts off a piece of a leaf.
The ant's jaw works like a saw.
Then, the ant lifts the leaf above its head.
All of the ants carry their leaves back to the nest.
Other ants in the nest chew the leaves.
They chew until the leaves are like paste.
The ants put the paste on some fungus.
The paste helps the fungus grow into ant food.

Fill in the circle next to the correct answer.

1. After the ants climb onto the leaves, _____.
   Ⓐ they chew the leaves
   Ⓑ they pull off the leaves
   Ⓒ they cut off pieces of leaves

2. Before they carry the leaves, _____.
   Ⓐ the ants lift the leaves high
   Ⓑ the ants place the leaves on fungus
   Ⓒ the ants chew up the leaves

3. What is the first job of the ants in the nest?
   Ⓐ They put the leaves on some fungus.
   Ⓑ They chew the leaves.
   Ⓒ They hold the leaves with their jaws.

WORD MEANINGS

Circle where a jaw is.

   1. on the leg   2. on the hand   3. on the face

Name: _____

WEEK 21
Sequence DAY 5

Read the story. Ask yourself, "What happened each summer?"

Last summer was my first time at Camp Kickapoo.
I was a little afraid, so I took Bosco with me.
Bosco is my stuffed monkey.
This summer I am back at camp.
I left Bosco at home.
I am learning how to dive.
I am getting good at swimming, too.
Next summer at camp, I will get to row a boat.
I will learn how to use the oars.
I will row while the boat is tied to the pier.
Then, I will row the boat on the lake.

Fill in the circle next to the correct answer.

1. What is the boy doing at camp this summer?
   Ⓐ rowing a boat
   Ⓑ learning to dive
   Ⓒ taking Bosco along

2. When will the boy learn to row a boat?
   Ⓐ next summer
   Ⓑ this summer
   Ⓒ last summer

3. What will the boy do while the boat is tied to the pier?
   Ⓐ learn to swim in the lake
   Ⓑ learn to use the oars
   Ⓒ learn to dive off the pier

WORD MEANINGS

Circle the pier.

1.    2.    3.

© Evan-Moor Corp. • EMC 3451 • Daily Reading Comprehension

WEEK 22

Compare and Contrast

Students practice Compare and Contrast *by looking at the similarities and differences between two people or things.*

DAY 1

Say: **This week we will practice the reading skill *Compare and Contrast*, telling how people or things are the same and how they are different.** Direct students' attention to the illustration, and read the instructions at the top of the page aloud. Read the first sentence of the story. Ask: **Does this sentence tell what is the same about lions and tigers or what is different?** (same) Read through sentence four. Ask: **What is different about where lions and tigers live?** Read through sentence eight. Ask: **What is different about the ways lions and tigers hunt?** Read the remaining sentences. Ask: **What is different about the way lions and tigers feel about water?** Guide students through the first activity, letting them give a thumbs up or a thumbs down to each answer choice. Look back at the story for clues if there are disagreements about the correct answers. Instruct students to complete the phonics activity with a partner.

DAY 2

Say: **Today we will read about two brothers named Jonah and Nate and the kind of ice-cream treats they like to make.** Read the instructions aloud. Ask: **Would a Venn diagram help us remember what is the same and different about the boys?** (yes) Read the story once, and then reread it, making a Venn diagram of the facts. Keep the entries simple. (Nate—two scoops, fudge, letter *N* on top; Jonah—vanilla cone, cookie crumbs, whipped cream, gumball) Have students look at the picture and label whose ice cream it is. (Nate's) Then guide them through the first activity. Have them circle the key word in each item *(same, different, same)* before considering the answer choices. Refer to the Venn diagram as you do the activity. Give students the option of doing the phonics activity independently or with a partner.

DAY 3

Review the skill. Say: **Today we are going to read about goats and sheep.** Read the instructions aloud. Then say: **As we read, underline every sentence that tells how the animals are the same. Circle every sentence that tells how the animals are different.** Read the story slowly, allowing students time to mark the sentences appropriately. After reading, lead students in doing the first activity. Show how they can refer back to the sentences they underlined and circled for help. Complete the phonics activity together.

DAY 4

Remind students of the skill. Then read the instructions aloud. Say: **Good readers can do things to help themselves remember what they read. They can underline. They can make a Venn diagram. They can make a chart.** Make a two-column chart on the board with *Whales* as one head and *Fish* as the other. Read the story. Have students raise their hands when they hear a fact to write in the chart. Keep the entries short and simple. Refer to the chart as an aide while completing the first activity. Allow students to do the phonics activity independently or with a partner.

DAY 5

Read the instructions aloud. Ask students to provide words to tell what they will be doing. (comparing and contrasting) Read the story and guide students in underlining what is the same about Sasha and Adam. (backpacks, milk and a snack, work at kitchen table) Guide students through the first activity slowly, making sure they understand the items. Instruct students to complete the phonics activity independently.

Name: _____

Compare and Contrast

WEEK 22 DAY 1

Read the story. Find out how lions and tigers are the same and different.

Lions and tigers are big, wild cats.
They live in different places in the world.
Lions live in grasslands.
Tigers live where there are a lot of trees.
Lions and tigers are strong hunters.
They hunt mostly at night.
A tiger lives and hunts by itself.
Lions live in families and hunt in groups.
Tigers like to cool off in water.
But lions try to stay dry.
Lions and tigers both like to roar.

Fill in the circle next to the correct answer.

1. How is a lion different from a tiger?
   Ⓐ A lion is a wild cat, but a tiger is not.
   Ⓑ A lion is a hunter, but a tiger is not.
   Ⓒ A lion lives in a family, but a tiger does not.

2. Which one tells about lions and tigers?
   Ⓐ They hunt at night.
   Ⓑ They like to swim.
   Ⓒ They live in grassy lands.

3. How are tigers and lions different?
   Ⓐ A tiger is a hunter, but a lion is not.
   Ⓑ A tiger roars, but a lion does not.
   Ⓒ A tiger hunts by itself, but a lion does not.

VOWEL SOUNDS

The vowel sound you hear in <u>moon</u> may be spelled with <u>oo</u> or <u>ou</u>.
Circle two words in the story that have the same vowel sound as <u>moon</u>.

Name: _____

Compare and Contrast

WEEK 22 DAY 2

Read the story. Ask yourself how Jonah and Nate are the same and different.

> Jonah and Nate love Sundays in the summer.
> On Sundays, Gramps takes the boys for ice cream.
> The boys make their own ice-cream treats.
> Nate piles two scoops into a dish.
> He pours fudge on top.
> Then he makes a big letter **N** with whipped cream.
> Jonah likes ice-cream cones.
> He starts with a scoop of vanilla.
> Then he spoons on some cookie crumbs.
> He squirts on some whipped cream, too.
> Jonah ends with a gum ball on top.

Fill in the circle next to the correct answer.

1. What is the same about the boys?
   - Ⓐ They like vanilla ice cream best.
   - Ⓑ They eat ice-cream cones.
   - Ⓒ They make ice-cream treats.

2. How are the treats different?
   - Ⓐ Jonah puts the ice cream in a dish, but Nate does not.
   - Ⓑ Jonah puts a gum ball on top, but Nate does not.
   - Ⓒ Jonah likes whipped cream, but Nate does not.

3. What is the same about Nate's and Jonah's ice-cream treats?
   - Ⓐ Gramps makes the treats for both boys.
   - Ⓑ Both boys put the ice cream in a dish.
   - Ⓒ Both boys use whipped cream.

VOWEL SOUNDS

Circle the two letters in each word that together spell the long e sound.

1. treat
2. cookie
3. cream
4. piece

Name: _____

Compare and Contrast WEEK 22 DAY 3

Read the story. Find out how sheep and goats are the same and different.

Sheep and goats are the same in some ways.
People think both animals are good to eat.
People like to drink their milk, too.
Their milk often is made into soft cheese.
Sheep and goats look different.
Goats have beards, but sheep do not.
The tail of a goat goes up.
A sheep's tail hangs down.
Most sheep have thick, curly fur called wool.
Goats have short or long hair.
Both a sheep's wool and a goat's hair are
   made into yarn.

Fill in the circle next to the correct answer.

1. How are goats and sheep the same?
   Ⓐ They both have curly wool.
   Ⓑ They both have beards.
   Ⓒ They both give milk.

2. How is a sheep different from a goat?
   Ⓐ A sheep does not have a beard, but a goat does.
   Ⓑ A sheep is good to eat, but a goat is not.
   Ⓒ A sheep's wool is made into yarn, but a goat's hair is not.

3. How is a goat different from a sheep?
   Ⓐ A goat's tail goes down, but a sheep's tail does not.
   Ⓑ A goat's tail goes up, but a sheep's tail does not.
   Ⓒ A goat has a tail, but a sheep does not.

LONG VOWEL SOUNDS

Circle five words in the story that have a long e sound.

Name: _____

Compare and Contrast **WEEK 22 DAY 4**

Read the story. Find out how whales and fish are the same and different.

Whales and fish both live and swim in water.
But whales are not fish.
Baby fish hatch from eggs.
But baby whales are born live.
Whales and fish swim in different ways.
Whales move their tails up and down.
Fish move their tails from side to side.
Whales and fish do not breathe in the same way.
Fish can breathe underwater.
But whales are like people.
They need air to breathe.

Fill in the circle next to the correct answer.

1. Which one tells about both whales and fish?
   - Ⓐ They both live in water.
   - Ⓑ They both hatch from eggs.
   - Ⓒ They both breathe underwater.

2. Which fact shows that whales are not fish?
   - Ⓐ Whales swim in water.
   - Ⓑ Whales breathe air.
   - Ⓒ Whales move their tails to swim.

3. How are whales different from fish?
   - Ⓐ Whales cannot move their tails, but fish can.
   - Ⓑ Whales move their tails up and down, but fish do not.
   - Ⓒ Whales move their tails from side to side, but fish do not.

VOWEL SOUNDS

Circle the letter that spells the <u>vowel sound</u> you hear in each word.

1. tail a i
2. like e i
3. breathe e a

Name: _____

Compare and Contrast

WEEK 22 DAY 5

Read the story. What do the children do that is the same and different?

Sasha and Adam go home after school.
Adam throws his backpack on the kitchen floor.
Then he pours himself a glass of milk.
He eats a snack while he plays a game.
Sasha tosses her backpack on her bed.
She gets herself a glass of milk and a snack.
Then Sasha starts her homework.
She likes to finish her homework before supper.
Adam needs a break after school.
He does his homework after supper.
They both work at the kitchen table.

Fill in the circle next to the correct answer.

1. Which one is true about Adam?
   Ⓐ He puts his backpack on his bed.
   Ⓑ He takes a break after school.
   Ⓒ He does his homework before supper.

2. What do Adam and Sasha do before supper that is the same?
   Ⓐ They both do their homework.
   Ⓑ They both drink milk.
   Ⓒ They both play games.

3. What does Sasha do after school that is different from Adam?
   Ⓐ Sasha plays a game, but Adam does not.
   Ⓑ Sasha eats a snack, but Adam does not.
   Ⓒ Sasha does her homework before supper, but Adam does not.

ENDING SOUNDS

Circle the letter that spells the sound you hear at the <u>end</u> of each word.

1. pours   s   z

2. glass   s   z

WEEK 23

Author's Purpose

With Author's Purpose, *students identify why an author wrote a story. Students learn that an author may write to tell a fun story, to give information, or to tell how to do something.*

DAY 1

Recall for students that an author is the person who writes a story. Tell students that this week they will practice a reading skill called finding the *Author's Purpose,* or why an author wrote a story. Say: **Sometimes the author wants to make you laugh with a fun story. Sometimes the author wants to teach you some facts. Sometimes the author wants to explain how to do something. Today we will read a story about jungles. The instructions at the top of the page will tell us what to find as we read.** Read the instructions at the top of the page aloud, and then read the story as students follow along. Then reread the story slowly as students read with you. Guide them through the first activity, considering each answer choice for each item and talking about its appropriateness as the correct response. For item 1, ask students to tell a partner one fact about an animal in the story. Then ask students to complete the sight words activity with a partner.

DAY 2

Recall the story from Day 1 and why the author wrote it. (to tell about some jungle animals) Say: **The flying squirrel is one animal the author wrote about. Today we will read a story that tells more about flying squirrels.** Read the instructions aloud. Then read the story as students follow along or read with you. Call attention to the illustration. Say: **Pictures can help you understand what you read.** To understand the value of an illustration, have students explain the picture to a partner. Then lead students through the first activity. Let them complete the sight words activity independently. Some students may find it useful to read the letters out loud as they write them.

DAY 3

Remind students of the Day 2 story about flying squirrels. Say: **Do you remember why the author wrote that story? Was it "to show you how to fly like a squirrel," "to tell about flying squirrels," or "to laugh at squirrels"?** (to tell about flying squirrels) **The author's purpose of both stories this week was to tell you information about something.** Read the instructions aloud. Then say: **Let's see if the author's purpose of this story is the same or different.** Read the story as students follow along or read with you. Guide them in completing the first activity. Let students find silly or funny elements in the story that indicate the author wanted to tell a fun story. Ask students to complete the sight words activity with a partner.

DAY 4

Recall with students the three stories read this week and the reasons the authors wrote those stories. Write the reasons on the board. (to tell facts, to tell facts, to tell a fun story) Then direct students' attention to the numbered steps of today's story. Have students use the steps as a clue as to why the author probably wrote this story. (to tell how to do something) Then read the instructions aloud. Read the story, with students reading along. After reading, have students recap the story by explaining the illustration to a partner. Then lead students in completing the first activity. Instruct them to complete the sight words activity independently.

DAY 5

Review the three reasons an author writes a story—to tell a fun story, to tell facts, to tell how to do something. Then read the instructions at the top of the page aloud. Read the story slowly and carefully, pausing and showing students how to refer to the illustration to understand the facts. Then guide students in completing the first activity. Instruct them to do the sight words activity with a partner, reading the words out loud.

Name: _____

Author's Purpose — WEEK 23, DAY 1

Read the story. Ask yourself, "Why did the author write this story?"

Rain falls almost every day in jungles.
Plants and trees grow fast.
The tops of tall trees grow close together.
Animals can go from tall tree to tall tree.
Some of the animals glide to do this.
A flying squirrel stretches some skin.
Then the squirrel can glide like a kite.
A flying frog has skin between its toes.
It opens its four feet like umbrellas.
A flying tree snake jumps from a tree.
It makes its body flat so it can glide in the air.

Fill in the circle next to the correct answer.

1. Why did the author write the story?
   Ⓐ to make you laugh
   Ⓑ to tell you about some jungle animals
   Ⓒ to tell you how to draw a jungle

2. How does a flying snake glide?
   Ⓐ It uses an umbrella.
   Ⓑ It spreads its skin.
   Ⓒ It makes its body flat.

3. What does the author tell you about jungles?
   Ⓐ Jungles are hot all the time.
   Ⓑ Jungles are very dry.
   Ⓒ Jungles get a lot of rain.

SIGHT WORDS

Circle the word that correctly completes the sentence.

My dog can jump (open   over) a puddle of water.

Name: _____

Author's Purpose — WEEK 23 DAY 2

Read the story. Ask yourself, "Why did the author write this story?"

A flying squirrel does not really fly.
It glides through the air.
First, it stands on a branch.
It pushes off with its back legs.
Then, it spreads all four legs.
A flying squirrel has loose skin between
   its front and back legs.
The skin stretches when the legs spread.
Then the squirrel's body looks like a kite.
Off it goes! The squirrel soars through the air.
It lands gently on the branch of another tree.

Fill in the circle next to the correct answer.

1. Why did the author write the story?
   Ⓐ to show how to fly like a squirrel
   Ⓑ to tell about flying squirrels
   Ⓒ to laugh at squirrels

2. Which one helps a flying squirrel to glide?
   Ⓐ two thin wings
   Ⓑ a fat body
   Ⓒ skin that stretches

3. What does the author tell you about flying squirrels?
   Ⓐ They are as big as cats.
   Ⓑ They use wings to fly.
   Ⓒ They glide but do not fly.

SIGHT WORDS

Write the letters on the lines to spell the word <u>through</u>.

1. thr __ __ gh   2. thr __ __ __ __   3. __ __ __ __ __ gh

Name: _____

Author's Purpose — WEEK 23 DAY 3

Read the story. Ask yourself, "Why did the author write this story?"

Booboo was the saddest clown you ever saw.
"Let us fix your frown," said some kids.
Carla turned upside down.
Mazy the cat danced in a gown.
Popeye the dog juggled balls of brown.
Travis wore a marshmallow crown.
But Booboo's mouth still stayed down.
Then Popeye gave the clown a lick.
And Mazy jumped onto his lap.
Carla and Travis said, "We will be your friends."
Booboo was as happy as could be!
There was no more frown for Booboo the clown.

Fill in the circle next to the correct answer.

1. Why did the author write the story?
   Ⓐ to tell a fun story
   Ⓑ to tell you about clowns
   Ⓒ to teach you how to smile

2. Which word best describes the story?
   Ⓐ silly
   Ⓑ scary
   Ⓒ true

3. Which sentence makes the story funny?
   Ⓐ "Mazy jumped onto his lap."
   Ⓑ "Booboo was as happy as could be!"
   Ⓒ "Travis wore a marshmallow crown."

SIGHT WORDS

Circle the two words that are the same.

1. met   2. let   3. let   4. left   5. led

Name: _____

Author's Purpose WEEK 23 DAY 4

Read the story. Ask yourself, "Why did the author write this story?"

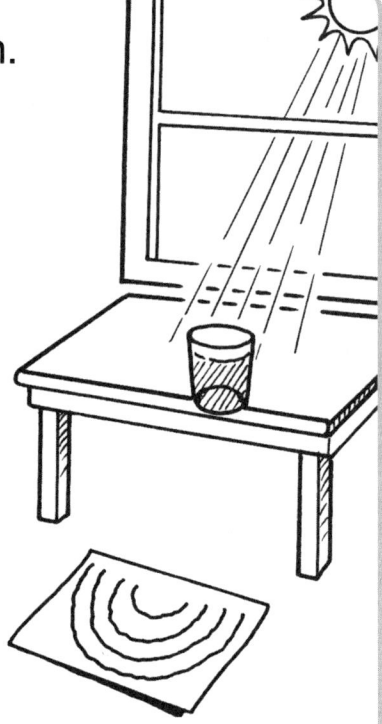

Sometimes, the sun shines through drops of rain.
Then the sunlight makes a rainbow.
You can make a rainbow indoors.
You will need the sun and some water.
Follow these steps:

1. Fill a glass with water, almost to the top.
2. Find a sunny window with a table in front.
3. Place the glass halfway off the table.
   Make sure the sun shines through the glass.
4. Place a white sheet of paper on the floor.
5. Slowly move the paper and the glass.
   Stop when a rainbow forms on the paper.

Fill in the circle next to the correct answer.

1. Why did the author write the story?
   Ⓐ to explain all about rainbows
   Ⓑ to tell you how to make a rainbow
   Ⓒ to tell you how to draw a rainbow

2. What makes a rainbow?
   Ⓐ sun and water
   Ⓑ paper and water
   Ⓒ sun and paper

3. The author numbered the steps _____.
   Ⓐ to show how to count
   Ⓑ to explain the picture
   Ⓒ to show the order to do things

SIGHT WORDS

Write the letters on the lines to spell the word <u>white</u>.

1. ___ ___ite   2. wh___ ___ ___   3. whit___

Name: _____

Author's Purpose — WEEK 23, DAY 5

Read the story. Ask yourself, "Why did the author write this story?"

> Beavers cut down trees to get their food.
> They eat all parts of a tree.
> Beavers have four very long front teeth.
> These teeth are made for cutting.
> The front teeth have a hard, strong coating.
> The coating turns the front teeth a bright orange.
> A beaver's orange front teeth always grow.
> So they stay strong and long.
> They keep a beaver from getting hungry!

Fill in the circle next to the correct answer.

1. Why did the author write the story?
   Ⓐ to make you laugh about beavers
   Ⓑ to tell you about beavers' teeth
   Ⓒ to explain how to cut down a tree

2. Beavers cut down trees because _____.
   Ⓐ they like to work hard
   Ⓑ they want to get food
   Ⓒ their teeth are orange

3. What does the author tell you about beavers' teeth?
   Ⓐ All of their teeth are white.
   Ⓑ Their front teeth are long and strong.
   Ⓒ Their teeth are soft and weak.

SIGHT WORDS

Circle the two words that are the same.

1. how   2. have   3. here   4. have   5. his

© Evan-Moor Corp. • EMC 3451 • Daily Reading Comprehension   147

WEEK 24

Prediction

With Prediction, *students use clues from a story and prior knowledge to predict what will happen next. Students understand that good predictions follow logically from the events of the story.*

DAY 1

Tell students that this week they will practice the reading skill *Prediction*. Say: **To predict means to make a good guess about what may happen next. Good readers pay close attention to what characters say and do. They use these clues to predict what will happen next.** Read the instructions at the top of the page aloud. Then read the story as students follow along or read with you. After reading, have students tell some of Mom's actions. Then lead students in completing the first activity. Have them refer to story facts to determine the answers. Complete the word meanings activity together. One at a time, read the sentences that begin with *Mom, She,* or *Then she*. Ask students to name the action word. Ask them if it tells a way that Mom picked her vegetables. Students will circle *tore, snipped, tugged,* and *plucked*. Then invite them to act out each action word.

DAY 2

Review the skill by recalling the prediction made about Mom in her garden in the story for Day 1. (Mom will probably make a salad for lunch.) Ask students to recall Mom's actions that were clues to making the prediction. (It was lunchtime. Mom tore off lettuce, snipped peas, pulled out a carrot, and plucked a tomato.) Say: **Today we will make predictions about a boy named Marc who saves things.** Read the instructions aloud. Then read the story as students follow along or read with you. Ask students to name the items Marc collects. (rocks and stones, feathers, tree bark, bird nest) Then lead students through item 1 of the first activity. Before answering item 2, reread the last three sentences in the story, and encourage students to make a prediction of what Marc may find to save. Instruct students to complete the word meanings activity independently. Allow for sharing of responses.

DAY 3

Review the skill by asking students to explain to a partner what *Prediction* means. Remind students to carefully read what characters say and do because these are clues as to what will probably happen next. Then read the instructions aloud. Read the story as students follow along or read with you. After reading, guide students through the first activity. Help students find and read parts of the story that support their answer choices. Do the word meanings activity together. Reread each story sentence and then pause. Have students give a thumbs up if they heard a word that means to go fast. (*whooshed, zipped, zoomed*) As each correct word is said, write it on the board. Let students work with a partner to find and circle the three words in the story.

DAY 4

Tell students that today's story is about a girl named Izzy and her loose tooth. Remind students of the skill by saying: **To make a prediction, pay attention to what Izzy does in the story. You also can use what you know about loose teeth to help you predict what will happen next.** Read the instructions and the story as students follow along or read with you. After reading, lead them in completing the first activity. For item 1, ask how they know what will happen next. For item 3, have students suggest the key words (*very loose*) before determining the correct answer. Instruct students to do the word meanings activity independently. Share student responses.

DAY 5

Direct students' attention to the illustration. Tell them the boy is named Lamar and that the story is about the house next door to him. Read the instructions aloud. Then read the story as students follow along. Help students complete the first activity. They should be able to provide clues from the story to support their answers. Do the word meanings activity together. Then ask students to name other things that can creak.

Name: _____

Prediction — **WEEK 24 DAY 1**

Read the story. Ask yourself, "What will probably happen next?"

Mom saw that it was time for lunch.
She took her basket into the garden.
Mom liked to pick her vegetables.
She tore off a bunch of lettuce leaves.
They went on the bottom of the basket.
Then she snipped off some pea pods.
They fell into the basket with a plunk.
Mom then looked at the carrot tops.
She tugged at the greenest one.
Out came an orange carrot.
Some of the tomatoes were small and green.
Mom plucked a red tomato that smelled good.

Fill in the circle next to the correct answer.

1. What will Mom probably do next?
   Ⓐ make a salad for lunch
   Ⓑ make a sandwich for supper
   Ⓒ buy lettuce at the market

2. Which one tells about Mom?
   Ⓐ She hates to eat vegetables.
   Ⓑ She sells vegetables.
   Ⓒ She likes to grow a garden.

3. What will probably happen when more tomatoes turn red?
   Ⓐ Mom will let them rot.
   Ⓑ Mom will pick them to eat.
   Ⓒ Mom will throw them away.

WORD MEANINGS

Look back at the story.
Circle the four action words that tell the ways Mom picked her vegetables.

© Evan-Moor Corp. • EMC 3451 • Daily Reading Comprehension

Name: _____

Prediction **WEEK 24 DAY 2**

Read the story. Ask yourself, "What will probably happen next?"

The table in Marc's room is full of stuff.
Marc saves things that he finds outside.
Bumpy rocks sit next to flat stones.
Bird feathers are in a pile.
Pieces of tree bark are in a row.
A small bird nest is near the bark.
Marc found the nest on the grass in the park.
Marc is making a space on the table.
Today he will go to the beach!
He will find something new to save.

Fill in the circle next to the correct answer.

1. What does Marc save?
   Ⓐ things he buys
   Ⓑ things he makes
   Ⓒ things he finds outside

2. What will Marc most likely put on the table after he goes to the beach?
   Ⓐ some seashells
   Ⓑ some books
   Ⓒ some socks

3. Which place would Marc be most likely to look for other things to save?
   Ⓐ in his yard
   Ⓑ at the library
   Ⓒ in the supermarket

WORD MEANINGS

On the line, write something you see in the room that is <u>bumpy</u>.

_____

Name: _____

Prediction **WEEK 24 DAY 3**

Read the story. Ask yourself, "What will probably happen next?"

> Once there was a fox that ran very fast.
> Fox bragged, "No one is faster than I am!"
> He liked to dare other animals to race.
> Fox always won.
> He whooshed past the snake.
> He zipped past the squirrel.
> Fox even zoomed past the quick white rabbit.
> Snail was the one animal Fox had not raced.
> Snail carried a heavy shell on her back.
> She had only one foot.
> And she moved very slowly.
> One day, Snail was tired of hearing Fox brag.
> Snail said, "I will race you, Fox."

Fill in the circle next to the correct answer.

1. What will Fox probably say to Snail?
   - Ⓐ "No, thanks. You are too fast for me."
   - Ⓑ "Sure. Beating you will be easy."
   - Ⓒ "I am busy. I have no time to race."

2. Who would probably win a race between Fox and Snail?
   - Ⓐ Snail would beat Fox.
   - Ⓑ Fox and Snail would tie.
   - Ⓒ Fox would be the winner.

3. What will probably happen if Fox wins the race?
   - Ⓐ He will tell Snail he is sorry.
   - Ⓑ He will stop racing.
   - Ⓒ He will act like a showoff.

WORD MEANINGS

Circle three action words in the story that tell that Fox went fast.

© Evan-Moor Corp. • EMC 3451 • Daily Reading Comprehension

Name: _____

Prediction WEEK 24 DAY 4

Read the story. Ask yourself, "What will probably happen next?"

Izzy hummed while she brushed her teeth.
Toothpaste dripped out of her mouth.
Then Izzy suddenly stopped.
Izzy placed her brush by the sink.
She gently touched a front tooth with her finger.
Sure enough, the tooth wiggled.
The tooth went back and forth like a rocking chair.
The day passed by.
Izzy didn't think about her loose tooth.
She forgot about it, even when she bit into
  an apple.

Fill in the circle next to the correct answer.

1. What will probably happen next?
   Ⓐ Izzy's tooth will come out in the apple.
   Ⓑ Izzy will brush her loose tooth.
   Ⓒ Izzy will push her loose tooth back in.

2. What is the story mostly about?
   Ⓐ a girl and an apple
   Ⓑ a girl and toothpaste
   Ⓒ a girl and her loose tooth

3. Which sentence in the story tells that Izzy's tooth was very loose?
   Ⓐ "She gently touched a front tooth with her finger."
   Ⓑ "The tooth went back and forth like a rocking chair."
   Ⓒ "Then Izzy suddenly stopped."

WORD MEANINGS

On the line, write something else that can <u>wiggle</u>.

_____

Name: _____   Prediction   WEEK 24 DAY 5

Read the story. Ask yourself, "What will probably happen next?"

The house next door to Lamar's house was empty.
The paint was peeling, and the stairs creaked.
Lamar had lost a ball in the tall grass.
Then one day, loud noises came from the house.
Lamar looked over the fence.
Men were fixing the stairs.
Painters were painting the house a light blue.
A man walked up to Lamar.
"Is this your ball?" asked the man.
Soon after, a big van parked in front of the house.
Men unloaded boxes and crates.
One man carried a boy's bike.

Fill in the circle next to the correct answer.

1. What will probably happen next?
   Ⓐ The men will bring the boxes into Lamar's house.
   Ⓑ People will move into the empty house.
   Ⓒ People will move into Lamar's house.

2. Who will probably live next door?
   Ⓐ a boy and his family
   Ⓑ a family with many children
   Ⓒ a girl and her family

3. What kind of van parked in front of the empty house?
   Ⓐ a van full of food
   Ⓑ a moving van
   Ⓒ a van selling furniture

WORD MEANINGS

Circle what is meant by "the stairs creaked."

1. The stairs squeaked.   2. The stairs needed paint.

© Evan-Moor Corp. • EMC 3451 • Daily Reading Comprehension   153

WEEK 25

Main Idea and Details

Students read to understand the central message of a passage or story. They also monitor their comprehension of important details.

DAY 1

Tell students that this week they will practice the reading skill *Main Idea and Details*. Say: **Every story and every poem has a main idea, which is what the story or poem is about. Stories and poems also have details that tell more about the main idea.** If you wish, have students recall the main idea of a story read recently in class. Then read the instructions at the top of the page aloud. Remind students that the main idea is often given at the beginning of a story or poem. Read the poem aloud once or twice with students. After reading, guide them in completing the first activity by analyzing each answer choice. Help students refer to the text to determine the correct responses. Then do the phonics activity. Divide the class into three groups, with each group reading one verse of the poem out loud as the others follow along. After each verse is read, give students time to circle the two rhyming words. Discuss the rhyming pattern if appropriate.

DAY 2

Remind students of the skill. Tell them that today's story is nonfiction. If necessary, recall that nonfiction stories are facts about real people or things. Read the instructions aloud. Say: **Remember that the main idea is often at the beginning of a story. Good readers want to find the main idea as soon as they can to help them understand what they are reading.** Then read the story aloud as students follow along. Stop after the first three sentences and ask them to tell the main idea to a partner. (Three different shapes of teeth help you eat your food.) Share their responses, helping them to refine the verbiage. Finish reading the story. Ask if the rest of the story had the same main idea. (yes) Then lead students through the first activity, considering one answer choice at a time. For items 2 and 3, have students circle the key words. *(sharp, chew)* Tell students to find those words in the story to locate the information asked for in the items. Instruct students to do the phonics activity out loud with a partner. Review how the context of a sentence is a clue for pronouncing homonyms.

DAY 3

Review the skill by asking questions that students answer with a thumbs up for *yes* or a thumbs down for *no*. **Does the main idea tell what a story or poem is about?** (yes) **Does a nonfiction story have a main idea?** (yes) Then read the instructions aloud. Read the story as students follow along or read with you. After reading, guide students in completing the first activity. For item 1, remind students that what a story is mostly about is the main idea. For items 2 and 3, recall that stories give details about the main idea. Instruct students to complete the phonics activity independently.

DAY 4

Instruct students to explain *Main Idea* to a partner. Tell students that today's story is nonfiction and begins with a riddle. Read the instructions aloud. Then read the first paragraph as students follow along or read with you. Then pause and ask: **What animal is this story about?** (the panda) **What is the main idea of the first paragraph?** (what pandas eat) Then read the second paragraph and lead students in determining its main idea. (facts about baby pandas) Guide students in completing the first activity. Do the phonics activity together.

DAY 5

Tell students that today they will read a story about a boy named Hank and his pet snake named Hose. Recall: **All stories have a main idea. The main idea is what the story is *mostly* about.** Then read the instructions aloud. Read the story and guide students in completing the first activity. Have them refer to story details to help determine the correct answers. Instruct students to complete the phonics activity independently.

Name: _____

Main Idea and Details — WEEK 25 DAY 1

Read the poem. Ask yourself, "What is this poem about?"

If you had a wish,
A wish just for you,
What would you wish
To be able to do?

Dive deep in the ocean?
Discover new stars?
Make every day summer?
Meet monsters on Mars?

Find a chest full of gold?
Eat tons of ice cream?
Have a pet giraffe?
Win games for your team?

Fill in the circle next to the correct answer.

1. What is the poem mostly about?
   Ⓐ how to make birthday wishes
   Ⓑ things you might wish to do
   Ⓒ real things a first-grader can do

2. What does the poem say about wishes?
   Ⓐ All wishes come true.
   Ⓑ Making wishes is scary.
   Ⓒ You can wish for anything.

3. Which wish in the poem might make you sick?
   Ⓐ "Eat tons of ice cream."
   Ⓑ "Find a chest full of gold."
   Ⓒ "Discover new stars."

RHYMING WORDS

In each verse, circle the two words that rhyme.

© Evan-Moor Corp. • EMC 3451 • Daily Reading Comprehension

Name: _____

Main Idea and Details

WEEK 25 DAY 2

Read the story. Ask yourself, "What is this story about?"

You have three kinds of teeth.
Each kind of tooth is a different shape.
Each shape helps you eat your food.
Your flat front teeth are good for biting into food.
Your pointy teeth are sharp.
They are good for tearing food.
Big teeth are at the back of your mouth.
They are wide and strong.
These big teeth mash food to make it smaller.
They are used for chewing food, too.

Fill in the circle next to the correct answer.

1. What is the story mostly about?
   Ⓐ using your front teeth to bite food
   Ⓑ how different-shaped teeth do different things
   Ⓒ why you need to care for your teeth

2. What is the job of your sharp teeth?
   Ⓐ to chew food
   Ⓑ to bite into food
   Ⓒ to tear food

3. Which teeth do you use to chew?
   Ⓐ your big, wide teeth
   Ⓑ your sharp teeth
   Ⓒ your flat front teeth

VOWEL SOUNDS

Read each sentence out loud. Listen to how you say the underlined words.

1. I <u>read</u> that book last summer.

   Will you <u>read</u> me a story?

2. A <u>tear</u> rolled down the baby's cheek.

   Please do not <u>tear</u> my paper.

Name: _____

Main Idea and Details

WEEK 25 DAY 3

Read the story. Ask yourself, "What is this story about?"

Stella pressed her nose to the window.
The rain poured and poured.
Thunder rumbled.
Lightning flashed.
Stella had planned a picnic for today.
She and her dad had made pasta salad.
Stella had baked brownies all by herself.
The rain was spoiling everything.
Stella's dad walked into the room.
He said, "A picnic doesn't have to be outside.
  The living room floor is perfect for a picnic."
"You're right, Dad! No ants!" said Stella.

Fill in the circle next to the correct answer.

1. What is the story mostly about?
   Ⓐ thunder and lightning
   Ⓑ a dad cheering up his daughter
   Ⓒ a picnic being spoiled by rain

2. What will Stella and her dad eat at their picnic?
   Ⓐ brownies and sandwiches
   Ⓑ pasta salad and brownies
   Ⓒ sandwiches and cookies

3. Why does Stella think an indoor picnic is a good idea?
   Ⓐ The food will taste better.
   Ⓑ She and her dad will stay dry.
   Ⓒ The food will be safe from ants.

BASE WORDS AND ENDINGS

Underline the base word in each word below. Then circle the ending.

1. flashed   2. spoiling   3. says   4. walked

Name: _____

Main Idea and Details

WEEK 25 DAY 4

Read the story. Ask yourself, "What is this story about?"

What looks like a bear and makes noises like a sheep?
A giant panda!
There are very few pandas in the world.
They live only in bamboo forests.
Bamboo is a tall grass that looks like a thin tree.
Pandas eat lots of it.
They eat bamboo 12 hours a day.

Pandas are very small when they are born.
Baby pandas are about the size of a stick of butter.
Their skin is pink, and they have short white hair.
Then baby pandas get black spots on their skin.
Black fur will grow on those spots.

Fill in the circle next to the correct answer.

1. What is the story mostly about?
   Ⓐ what pandas eat
   Ⓑ facts about pandas
   Ⓒ bamboo forests

2. Which one is true about pandas?
   Ⓐ They growl like a bear.
   Ⓑ They can live anywhere.
   Ⓒ They eat for many hours during the day.

3. Which one is true about baby pandas?
   Ⓐ They first have black spots, and then they have black fur.
   Ⓑ They are born with some black fur and some white fur.
   Ⓒ They are very big when they are born.

CONSONANT SOUNDS

Circle the two letters at the beginning of each word that together spell the s blend.

1. small   2. skin   3. stick   4. spot

Name: _____

Main Idea and Details

WEEK 25 DAY 5

Read the story. Ask yourself, "What is this story about?"

Hank named his pet snake Hose.
The snake is green and long and thin.
Hose feels kind of like rubber, too.
Hank keeps Hose in a cage with a lid.
Hose has room to wiggle in the cage.
The snake can curl up to rest, too.
Like all snakes, Hose is wild.
Yesterday, Hose pushed the lid off the cage.
He slid along the floor.
Hank spent a long time looking for Hose.
He found his snake under a pile of papers.

Fill in the circle next to the correct answer.

1. What is the story mostly about?
   Ⓐ buying a pet snake
   Ⓑ having a pet snake
   Ⓒ saving a pet snake

2. What will Hank probably do next?
   Ⓐ make sure that Hose cannot get out of the cage
   Ⓑ leave Hose out of the cage
   Ⓒ give Hose a new name

3. Why is Hose a good name for the snake?
   Ⓐ It is full of water.
   Ⓑ It looks like a garden hose.
   Ⓒ It lives in the grass.

SYLLABLES

On the line, write the number of vowel sounds you hear in each word.

1. papers ___   2. along ___   3. cage ___   4. pile ___

© Evan-Moor Corp. • EMC 3451 • Daily Reading Comprehension

WEEK 26

Who, What, Where, and When

Students read to determine "who" (the main character), "what" (the main character's actions), "where" (the setting), and "when" (the time the story took place).

DAY 1

Write *Who, What, Where,* and *When* on the board. Point to each heading as you tell students that this week they will practice finding *Who* the main characters of a story are, *What* the characters do, *Where* the story takes place, and *When* the story happens. Then read the instructions at the top of the page aloud. Say: **The beginning of a story usually tells *who* the story is about. A story can have one main character or more than one. Let's read the story. Raise your hand when you hear who the story is about.** (Chuck, Aunt Tilly) After reading, lead students in answering the *what, where,* and *when* items that comprise the first activity. Have students use story details to support their answer choices. Instruct students to complete the sight words activity with a partner.

DAY 2

Review the skill by writing *Who, What, Where,* and *When* on the board. Ask students to explain what each word tells about a story. Read the instructions and the story aloud as students follow along or read with you. Stop after reading the third sentence. Ask: **Who is this story about?** (Jeb's family) **What do you think the rest of the story will tell us?** (what each family member does) Finish the story. Then guide students in doing the first activity. For items 2 and 3, have them tell story facts that are clues to the correct responses. Ask students to complete the sight words activity with a partner.

DAY 3

Read the instructions aloud. Then read the first two sentences. Pause and say: **Raise your hand if you think the story will be about the Fourth of July in a city named Whiting. What do you expect the rest of the story to tell?** (how people celebrate the Fourth of July in Whiting) Read the remainder of the story as students follow along or read with you. After reading, guide students in completing the first activity. The answer for item 2 depends on prior knowledge. Ask students to explain how they can determine the correct response. (The story takes place on July 4th, which is in the summer, so C is the answer.) Instruct students to complete the sight words activity independently. They may say the letters out loud as they write them.

DAY 4

Write *Who? What? Where?* and *When?* on the board. Then direct students' attention to the illustration. Say: **A picture often gives clues about the story. Which of these four questions does the picture probably answer?** (Who? Where?) Then read the instructions aloud. Read the story as students follow along or read with you. After reading, lead students in doing the first activity. Have them share story details that support the correct answers. Ask students to complete the sight words activity with a partner, reading the words out loud.

DAY 5

Say: **Today's story is nonfiction. Good readers use pictures to help them understand what they are reading. You can use these pictures to help you understand the facts of the story.** Then read the instructions aloud. Read the story as students follow along. After reading, have students show their understanding by labeling the *egg, nymph,* and *adult* in the illustration. Then guide students in completing the first activity and the sight words activity.

Name: _____

Who, What, Where, and When

WEEK 26 DAY 1

Read the story. Ask yourself, "Who? What? Where? When?"

Chuck stood near a window in his house.
He saw his Aunt Tilly drive up.
Chuck knew what would happen.
Aunt Tilly rushed inside.
"Chuckie!" she yelled.
Chuck's face turned red.
Aunt Tilly then hugged Chuck.
"Happy Birthday, Chuckie," she said.
She called him Chuckie all day long.
She smiled at him and patted his cheek.
Chuck liked the smiles.
But he did not like the nickname.

Fill in the circle next to the correct answer.

1. What makes Chuck's face turn red?
   Ⓐ His Aunt Tilly hugs him.
   Ⓑ His Aunt Tilly smiles at him.
   Ⓒ His Aunt Tilly calls him Chuckie.

2. Where does the story take place?
   Ⓐ at Aunt Tilly's house
   Ⓑ at Chuck's house
   Ⓒ in Aunt Tilly's truck

3. When does the story take place?
   Ⓐ on a Saturday
   Ⓑ on Aunt Tilly's birthday
   Ⓒ on Chuck's birthday

SIGHT WORDS

Circle the word that correctly completes the sentence.

I (saw   was) Aunt Tilly give Chuck a birthday gift.

Name: _____

Who, What, Where, and When

WEEK 26
DAY 2

Look at the picture. Read the story. Ask yourself, "Who? What? Where? When?"

The rooster crowed.
Jeb's family woke up.
Then everyone got busy.
Mother lit some candles.
Father grabbed a bucket.
He walked to the well to get some water.
Alice went to the chicken coop.
She picked up the fresh eggs.
Jeb chopped some wood.
Then he lit the wood to make a fire.
The fire quickly warmed the room.
Mother cut some bacon strips.
She fried them with the eggs over the fire.

Fill in the circle next to the correct answer.

1. What is Jeb's chore?
   Ⓐ He picks up the eggs.
   Ⓑ He cooks the food.
   Ⓒ He chops the wood.

2. Where does the story take place?
   Ⓐ in the country
   Ⓑ in a big city
   Ⓒ on the moon

3. When does the story take place?
   Ⓐ in the future
   Ⓑ long ago
   Ⓒ last week

SIGHT WORDS

Circle the two words that are the same.

1. want   2. what   3. walk   4. was   5. walk

Name: _____

Who, What, Where, and When

WEEK 26 DAY 3

Read the story. Ask yourself, "Who? What? Where? When?"

Whiting is a city by a lake.
The Fourth of July is a fun day in Whiting.
A parade marches down Main Street.
People stand and wave little flags.
Clowns toss candy to the kids.
Marchers beat drums and toot horns.
Families walk to the park after the parade.
They eat and play games.
At night, people drive to the lake.
They sit on blankets in the grass.
Fireworks sparkle in the sky.
Everyone goes to bed sleepy and happy.

Fill in the circle next to the correct answer.

1. What is the story mostly about?
   Ⓐ what a city does on July Fourth
   Ⓑ what songs horns play
   Ⓒ where people watch fireworks

2. When does the story take place?
   Ⓐ during the winter
   Ⓑ on the first day of school
   Ⓒ in the summer

3. Where does the story take place?
   Ⓐ in the city of Whiting
   Ⓑ in a park called Whiting
   Ⓒ on a lake named Whiting

SIGHT WORDS

Write the letters on the lines to spell the word <u>after</u>.

1. af __ __ __   2. __ fte __   3. af __ __ __

Daily Reading Comprehension • EMC 3451 • © Evan-Moor Corp.

Name: _____

Who, What, Where, and When

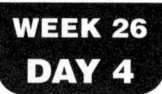

Read the story. Ask yourself, "Who? What? Where? When?"

Some second-graders were nervous.
And some looked a little scared.
This was their first day of school.
Then Miss Hobbs smiled.
She gave them each a seat.
Then she told the students about herself.
She showed her favorite books.
And she shared pictures of her cat.
The students played a name game.
They began to learn about each other.
After the game, the students made rules.
The rules would help them be kind.
By then, all of the second-graders were smiling.

Fill in the circle next to the correct answer.

1. Where does the story take place?
   Ⓐ in a classroom
   Ⓑ in a preschool
   Ⓒ at a ballgame

2. When does the story take place?
   Ⓐ on the first day of school
   Ⓑ on the last day of school
   Ⓒ on the second day of school

3. Who is the story about?
   Ⓐ first-graders and their teacher
   Ⓑ a teacher and her second-graders
   Ⓒ second-graders

SIGHT WORDS

Circle the two words that are the same.

1. his   2. this   3. her   4. this   5. that

Name: _____

Who, What, Where, and When — **WEEK 26 DAY 5**

Read the story. Ask yourself, "Who? What? Where? When?"

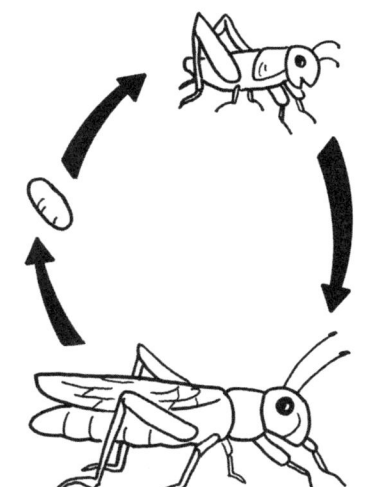

A grasshopper lays eggs in a hole.
Baby grasshoppers hatch in the spring.
The babies are called nymphs.
Nymphs are tiny grasshoppers without wings.
The nymphs grow bigger.
They get too big for their skin.
The nymphs shed their old skin.
Then they grow new skin.
Nymphs grow bigger and shed about five times.
Then they are adult grasshoppers.
Their legs are strong for hopping.
They have strong wings for flying.

Fill in the circle next to the correct answer.

1. What is the story mostly about?
   Ⓐ how grasshoppers lay eggs
   Ⓑ how nymphs change and grow
   Ⓒ how nymphs fly

2. Where does a grasshopper lay its eggs?
   Ⓐ in a hole
   Ⓑ in a tree
   Ⓒ in a nest

3. When do nymphs hatch?
   Ⓐ in the fall
   Ⓑ in the spring
   Ⓒ in the summer

SIGHT WORDS

Circle the word that correctly completes the sentence.

The (old   our) car makes a lot of noise.

Daily Reading Comprehension • EMC 3451 • © Evan-Moor Corp.

WEEK 27

Sequence

Students practice Sequence to determine the order of events or steps in a process.

DAY 1

Tell students that this week they will practice the reading skill called *Sequence*. Say: **Today's story tells the sequence—the order—in which a road is made. The story has signal words that make it easier to notice the order.** Read the instructions at the top of the page aloud. Instruct students to look through the story with a partner and circle the signal words. *(First, Then, Next, Finally)* Read the story as students follow along or read with you. After reading, ask students to name the three machines they read about (backhoe, dump truck, grader) and the job each does. Ask students to tell a partner the machine that is pictured on the page. (grader) Then guide students in completing the first activity by first circling the key words in each item *(first, When, last)*. Then read the word meanings activity aloud. Say: **A story often gives clues about what a word means. Let's find the word *grader* in the story and read about it.** Read the story sentence aloud and allow students a few moments to complete the activity.

DAY 2

Say: ***Sequence* is the order in which things happen.** Direct students' attention to the illustration and have them surmise what the story is about. Then read the instructions aloud. Ask: **What story clues can we look for that tell the order in which things go into the pot?** (signal words) Guide students in finding and circling the signal words. *(First, Then, Next, Then, Then, then)* Then read the story with students. After reading, ask: **What words in a question can help you understand what is asked?** (key words) Have students read an item, circle the key words *(right after, before, last thing)*, and then defend their answer choices, using facts from the story. Direct students to complete the word meanings activity independently. Share responses.

DAY 3

Say: ***Sequence* can tell the order in which you do something. Often, the order is given in steps. Each step can have a number. Why are numbers a good thing to have in directions?** Then read the instructions aloud. Call students' attention to the numbered steps in the story. Read the directions twice. The second time, divide the class in half, with one half reading the directions aloud and the other half following them. After reading, guide students in completing the first activity. Instruct students to complete the word meanings activity with a partner.

DAY 4

Remind students of the skill, and then read the instructions aloud. Tell students that today's story is nonfiction and has many facts. Suggest that they picture the steps in their mind as they read. Read the story as students follow along or read with you. Stop when necessary to help students clarify what is being read. When completing the first activity, guide students in circling the key word in an item *(After, then, Why)* before answering it. Instruct students to complete the word meanings activity independently and then check their answers with a partner.

DAY 5

Tell students that today's story, in some ways, is like the story of *Goldilocks and the Three Bears*. Then read the instructions aloud. Tell students to picture the story as they read it with you. Then guide them in completing the first activity, using key words in the items to help them. After students do the word meanings activity, ask them to tell clues in the story that helped them choose the right answer. (octopus swam; otters, crabs, and octopuses live in water)

Name: _____

Sequence **WEEK 27 DAY 1**

Read the story. Ask yourself, "What are the steps in making a road?"

Making a road takes a long time.
Large machines do most of the work.
First, a backhoe cleans up the land.
It digs up plants and dirt.
It scoops up heavy stones.
The backhoe drops the things into a dump truck.
The dump truck then drives the things away.
Then, someone tests the dirt.
The dirt needs to be strong.
Next, a machine called a grader smooths the dirt.
The dirt must be flat and packed tight.
Finally, trucks pour on a hard, black top layer.
That layer makes the road strong.

Fill in the circle next to the correct answer.

1. What is the first step in making a road?
   Ⓐ A grader makes the dirt flat and hard.
   Ⓑ A backhoe digs up stones and dirt.
   Ⓒ Trucks pour on a top layer.

2. When is the dirt tested?
   Ⓐ before stones and plants are dug up
   Ⓑ after a top layer is poured
   Ⓒ before the dirt is made smooth

3. What is the last step in making a road?
   Ⓐ A top layer is poured.
   Ⓑ Someone tests the dirt.
   Ⓒ Dump trucks take stones away.

WORD MEANINGS

Circle what a grader does.

1. digs rocks   2. makes the dirt flat   3. dumps things

Name: _____

Sequence **WEEK 27 DAY 2**

Read the story. Ask yourself, "In what order do things go into the pot?"

Lila likes to pretend that she's a cook.
She has a great big metal pot.
And she has a big wooden spoon.
Lila makes stew in the pot for her dolls.
First, she puts in a feather.
Then, she adds a few blocks.
Next, she sprinkles in some paper.
Then, she tosses in some rocks.
Lila stirs in three crayons.
Then, she squirts on some glue.
She mixes in buttons.
And then, she is through!

Fill in the circle next to the correct answer.

1. What does Lila put into the pot right after the rocks?
   Ⓐ some glue
   Ⓑ a feather
   Ⓒ three crayons

2. What is put in before the paper?
   Ⓐ blocks
   Ⓑ rocks
   Ⓒ crayons

3. What is the last thing Lila puts into the pot?
   Ⓐ a feather
   Ⓑ buttons
   Ⓒ glue

WORD MEANINGS

Write something you can:

1. toss _____   2. squirt _____   3. sprinkle _____

Name: _____

Sequence **WEEK 27 DAY 3**

Read the directions. Ask yourself, "What are the steps in playing this game?"

Play "Come to the Pond" with your friends.
One of you will be a pond animal.
The rest of you will be a pond.

1. Stand in a circle to form a pond.
   The pond animal stands in the middle.
2. The pond says, "Who is here to play today?"
3. The pond animal says the name of a pond animal.
4. The pond says, "How do you want to play today?"
5. The pond animal shows how it moves.
   For example, if the animal is a frog, he hops like a frog.
6. The pond moves like the pond animal.
7. Play again. Let a new player be a pond animal.

Fill in the circle next to the correct answer.

1. The pond animal says its name. What happens next?
   Ⓐ The pond animal hops like a frog.
   Ⓑ The players stand in a circle.
   Ⓒ The pond asks a question.

2. The pond moves in step _____.
   Ⓐ 6
   Ⓑ 7
   Ⓒ 2

3. Who asks a question first?
   Ⓐ the pond animal
   Ⓑ the pond
   Ⓒ the frog

WORD MEANINGS

Circle the word in the story that means center.

Name: _____

Sequence **WEEK 27 DAY 4**

Read the story. Find out the steps in getting milk from a farm to a store.

The milk you drink comes from a cow.
Every day, farmers milk their cows.
They send the milk to a dairy plant.
There, the milk is stored in large tanks.
The tanks keep the milk cold.
Next, the milk is quickly heated.
The heat gets rid of germs.
Then, the milk is made very cold again.
The cold milk is poured into large machines.
Milk cartons move along under the machines.
The machines pour the milk into the cartons.
Other machines close the tops.
Trucks take the cold milk to stores.

Fill in the circle next to the correct answer.

1. After a cow is milked, _____.
   Ⓐ the milk is put into large tanks
   Ⓑ the milk is heated
   Ⓒ the milk is poured into cartons

2. Machines pour milk into cartons, and then _____.
   Ⓐ the milk is put into trucks
   Ⓑ the tops of the cartons are closed
   Ⓒ the milk is heated

3. Why is milk heated?
   Ⓐ to make it taste good
   Ⓑ to make it easy to pour
   Ⓒ to get rid of germs

WORD MEANINGS

Circle what it means to "milk a cow."

   1. to pour milk into a cow
   2. to get milk out of a cow

Name: _____

Sequence **WEEK 27 DAY 5**

Read the story. Remember the order the octopus does things.

Ozzy was a rude octopus.
He swam right into the home of the three otters.
Ozzy saw three crabs lying on the table.
He took a bite of the big crab.
"This crab is too chewy!" said Ozzy.
Then he bit the middle-sized crab.
"This crab is too hard," he whined.
Ozzy bit the small crab and ate it all up.
Then Ozzy saw three pieces of kelp.
The big kelp was too long.
The middle-sized kelp was too stinky.
But the small kelp was just right.
Ozzy wrapped himself up and fell asleep.

Fill in the circle next to the correct answer.

1. The first thing Ozzy does in the otters' home is _____.
   Ⓐ bite the big crab
   Ⓑ eat the small crab
   Ⓒ wrap himself in kelp

2. What is the last thing Ozzy does?
   Ⓐ eat three pieces of crab
   Ⓑ leave the home of the otters
   Ⓒ fall asleep in some kelp

3. Which one is true about the middle-sized kelp?
   Ⓐ It is too stinky.
   Ⓑ It is too long.
   Ⓒ It is just right.

WORD MEANINGS

Circle where <u>kelp</u> grows.

1. on a farm   2. in the ocean   3. in a garden

WEEK 28

Compare and Contrast

Students practice Compare and Contrast *by looking at similarities and differences between two people or things.*

DAY 1

Say: **This week we will practice the reading skill *Compare and Contrast,* or telling how people or things are the same and how they are different. The picture shows us that the story has something to do with a sweater. Let's read to find out.** Read the instructions at the top of the page aloud. Have students read the story with you. Pause after reading line 8. Say: **We now know about one sweater. Let's write what we know to help us remember.** On the board, write students' suggestions in a column: *pink sweater, silver stars, size small, Cassie.* Finish reading the story. Then write facts about the other sweater in a column: *blue, gold stars, size medium, Nina.* Instruct students to complete the first activity on their own, referring to the information on the board for help. Check answers together. Allow students to explain their choices. Complete the phonics activity together.

DAY 2

Review the reading skill. Then say: **Today we will read a nonfiction story that compares and contrasts butterflies and moths.** Read the instructions aloud. Direct students' attention to the illustration. Say: **We can use this picture to help us understand the facts we will read.** Then read the first two sentences of the story with students. Determine whether the sentences tell what is the same about the two insects or what is different. (same) Read the next sentence and ask: **Will the next sentences probably tell us what is the same about the two bugs or what is different?** (different) Continue reading the story, pausing to refer to the illustration as an aide. After reading, tell students to label the moth and the butterfly in the picture based on the facts they read. Then guide students in completing the first activity, referring to the text and illustration when useful. Instruct students to complete the phonics activity independently and check their answers with a partner. Then check the responses.

DAY 3

Review the skill. Then read the instructions aloud. Say: **Good readers do things to help them understand a story. They can make a chart. They can look at the picture. They can make a Venn diagram. Today's story is about two girls and the foods they eat. Let's make a Venn diagram to help us remember what we read.** Draw the Venn diagram on the board. Title the sections *Jolie, Suri, Both.* Read the story as students follow along or read with you. After each sentence, decide if there are facts to enter on the diagram. After reading, lead students in completing the first activity, referring to the Venn diagram to confirm answer choices. For the phonics activity, have students use the method you have taught for determining the number of syllables in a word.

DAY 4

Remind students of the skill, and then read the instructions aloud. Pause after reading the first two story sentences to ask students if the sentences tell what is the same or what is different about Rico and Rob. (same) Finish reading the story. Then ask students to suggest what they can do to help remember the facts. (make a chart or a Venn diagram) Whichever method you use to recap the story, keep the entries short and simple. *(Rico, uses clay, makes a vase; Rob, paints a picture, makes a vase)* Allow students to complete the first activity independently or with a partner, referring to the visual aide for help. Check answers together. Complete the phonics activity together.

DAY 5

Ask students to help you give a very short synopsis of the story *Goldilocks and the Three Bears.* Then read the instructions aloud. Have the students read the story with you. Then guide them in completing the activities.

Name: _____

Compare and Contrast

WEEK 28 DAY 1

Read the story. Ask, "What is the same and different about the sweaters?"

Cassie and Nina are shopping.
They walk into their favorite store.
Nina sees a sweater that she likes.
The sweater is pink with silver stars.
Cassie likes the same sweater.
The girls begin to fight.
The sweater, however, is a small size.
It will fit Cassie.
Nina stomps over to another part of the store.
There she sees the same kind of sweater.
But that sweater is blue with gold stars.
The tag says the size is medium.
That sweater is just right for Nina.

Fill in the circle next to the correct answer.

1. What is the same about the sweaters?
   Ⓐ They are blue.
   Ⓑ They have stars.
   Ⓒ They are pink.

2. Which one tells about Cassie's sweater?
   Ⓐ It is a small size.
   Ⓑ It is a medium size.
   Ⓒ It is a large size.

3. How is Nina's sweater different from Cassie's?
   Ⓐ Nina's sweater is blue, but Cassie's is not.
   Ⓑ Nina's sweater has stars, but Cassie's does not.
   Ⓒ Nina's sweater is pink, but Cassie's is not.

BLENDS

Circle the two letters at the beginning of each word that spell the s blend.

1. sweater   2. store   3. small   4. skip

Name: _____

Compare and Contrast — WEEK 28, DAY 2

Read the story. Find out how butterflies and moths are the same and different.

Butterflies and moths have colorful wings.
And they both suck juice from flowers.
How can you tell moths and butterflies apart?
Take a look at each bug's body.
A butterfly's body is thin.
A moth has a chubby body.
Watch the bug rest.
A butterfly rests with its wings up.
A moth spreads its wings flat.
If you see the bug at night, it is a moth.
Butterflies fly during the day.

Fill in the circle next to the correct answer.

1. How are butterflies and moths alike?
   - Ⓐ They both fly during the day.
   - Ⓑ They both have chubby bodies.
   - Ⓒ They both eat juice from flowers.

2. How is a moth different from a butterfly?
   - Ⓐ A moth rests with its wings flat, but a butterfly does not.
   - Ⓑ A moth has colorful wings, but a butterfly does not.
   - Ⓒ A moth has a thin body, but a butterfly does not.

3. How is a butterfly different from a moth?
   - Ⓐ A butterfly eats juice from flowers, but a moth does not.
   - Ⓑ A butterfly is a flying bug, but a moth is not.
   - Ⓒ A butterfly flies during the day, but a moth does not.

PLURAL WORDS

Look back at the story. Circle four naming words that mean "more than one."

Name: _____

Compare and Contrast — WEEK 28 DAY 3

Read the story. Find out how the girls' lunches are the same and different.

Jolie and Suri sat at a picnic table.
Jolie unpacked her basket.
She ripped open a bag of chips.
She and Suri dunked the chips into some dip.
Then Suri shared some salad.
She brought the potato salad they both liked.
Jolie unwrapped her turkey sandwich.
She stuffed a big bite into her mouth.
Suri never eats meat.
She ate some cheese and carrots.
Jolie offered Suri some lemonade.
But Suri wanted to drink her juice.

Fill in the circle next to the correct answer.

1. What does Jolie eat that Suri does <u>not</u>?
   Ⓐ chips and dip
   Ⓑ turkey
   Ⓒ juice

2. What do both girls like to eat?
   Ⓐ turkey sandwiches
   Ⓑ lemonade
   Ⓒ potato salad

3. How is Suri's food different from Jolie's food?
   Ⓐ Suri has a drink, but Jolie does not.
   Ⓑ Suri brings carrots, but Jolie does not.
   Ⓒ Suri eats chips and dip, but Jolie does not.

SYLLABLES

Draw a line between the two syllables you hear in each word.

1. butter   2. carrots   3. apple

Name: _____

Compare and Contrast WEEK 28 DAY 4

Read the story. Ask, "What is the same and different about the boys?"

Rico and Rob like to create things.
They both go to an art center every Friday.
Last Friday, Rico played with clay.
He rolled a ball of clay until it was soft.
Then he stuck his thumb into the ball.
He pinched the clay with his fingers.
Before long, Rico shaped a small vase.
Rob stood in front of a big sheet of paper.
He made big strokes with a brush.
He splashed on bright colors.
Like Rico, Rob made a vase.
But Rob's vase could be put in a frame.

Fill in the circle next to the correct answer.

1. What is the same about Rob and Rico?
   Ⓐ They both paint pictures.
   Ⓑ They both make vases.
   Ⓒ They both play with clay.

2. Rico makes a clay vase, but Rob _____.
   Ⓐ colors a drawing of a vase
   Ⓑ paints a picture of a vase
   Ⓒ paints a wall with a brush

3. Which word describes both Rico and Rob?
   Ⓐ bored
   Ⓑ lazy
   Ⓒ creative

VOWEL SOUNDS

Circle the two letters in each word that have the same vowel sound you hear in <u>push</u>.

1. stood   2. could   3. foot

Name: _____

Compare and Contrast — WEEK 28 DAY 5

Read the story. How are the bears like real bears and how are they different?

> Goldilocks meets three bears in a fairy tale.
> Are the three bears like real bears?
> The three bears live in a house in the woods.
> Real bears live in the woods, too.
> But they also live in caves and trees.
> The three bears walk on their back legs.
> Real bears walk on all four legs.
> The three bears see the mess that Goldilocks made.
> Real bears cannot see very well.
> Goldilocks sees the three bears and runs away.
> All bears, even the make-believe bears, can be scary!

Fill in the circle next to the correct answer.

1. Which word describes real bears and the three bears?
   - Ⓐ scary
   - Ⓑ friendly
   - Ⓒ busy

2. What is true about real bears and the three bears?
   - Ⓐ They scare Goldilocks.
   - Ⓑ They live in the woods.
   - Ⓒ They can see very well.

3. How are real bears different from the three bears?
   - Ⓐ Real bears live in caves, but the three bears do not.
   - Ⓑ Real bears walk on two legs, but the three bears do not.
   - Ⓒ Real bears live in the woods, but the three bears do not.

LONG VOWEL SOUNDS

Circle three words in the story where y stands for the long e sound.

© Evan-Moor Corp. • EMC 3451 • Daily Reading Comprehension

WEEK 29

Author's Purpose

With Author's Purpose, students identify why an author wrote a story. Students learn that an author may write to tell a fun story, to give information, or to tell how to do something.

DAY 1

Have students explain what an author does. Tell students that this week they will practice a reading skill called finding the *Author's Purpose*, or why an author wrote a story. Recall with students some reasons authors write stories: to entertain/tell a fun story, to share facts, to tell how to do something. Invite students to suggest why it is good to know why an author wrote a story. Then read the instructions at the top of the page aloud to focus students on the purpose for reading. Have students read with you the directions for making butter. After reading, guide students in doing item 1 in the first activity. Allow them to explain their answer choices. After students complete items 2 and 3 independently, check their responses. If needed, clarify misconceptions or confusion about the story. Instruct students to complete the sight words activity independently.

DAY 2

Recall the story for Day 1 and why the author wrote it. (to tell how to make butter) Direct students' attention to the illustration on page 180 and ask them to guess what the story is about. (a spider) Read the instructions aloud. Read the first two sentences and pause to ask students what they expect the rest of the story to tell. (facts about the crab spider) Finish reading the story together. Then guide students in answering item 1 in the first activity by noticing that the story has many facts, and, therefore, the answer is C. Allow students to complete items 2 and 3 on their own. Check their responses and clarify misconceptions. Have students complete the sight words activity.

DAY 3

Ask students to explain *Author's Purpose* in their own words. Recall reasons why authors write stories. Then read the instructions and begin reading the story aloud together. Pause after the third sentence, and ask students to raise their hands if they think the story is nonfiction and will have many true facts about Bug and Hare. (no) Finish reading the story together. Then allow students time to do the first activity. Check their responses, encouraging them to use details from the story to support their answers. Instruct students to complete the sight words activity independently.

DAY 4

Review the reading skill. Then read the instructions on the page. Suggest to students that they picture what they are reading as you read the story together. After reading, ask students to identify the story as fiction or nonfiction to help them determine the author's purpose. (nonfiction) Give students time to complete the page. Check their responses. Encourage students to support their choices for the first activity with details from the story.

DAY 5

Review the three reasons why authors write stories. (to entertain the reader/tell a fun story, to tell facts, to tell how to do something) After reading the instructions aloud, have students read the story along with you. Allow time for them to complete the activities. Check their responses and clarify misconceptions or confusion.

Name: _____

Author's Purpose

WEEK 29
DAY 1

Read the directions. Ask yourself, "Why did the author write this story?"

Do you have whipping cream and a jar with a lid?
Then you can make butter!
First, pour whipping cream into the jar.
Fill the jar half full.
Next, put the lid on tight.
Then, shake the jar again and again.
Shake until you see some yellow lumps.
The lumps are the butter.
The liquid is buttermilk.
Pour out the buttermilk.
Then, rinse the butter in water.
The butter is ready for some hot toast.

Fill in the circle next to the correct answer.

1. Why did the author write the story?
   Ⓐ to tell you how to make butter
   Ⓑ to tell you all about butter
   Ⓒ to tell you how to make buttermilk

2. What do you need to make butter?
   Ⓐ buttermilk
   Ⓑ whipping cream
   Ⓒ milk and cream

3. Which sentence from the story is a step in making butter?
   Ⓐ "Then you can make butter!"
   Ⓑ "Pour out the buttermilk."
   Ⓒ "The liquid is buttermilk."

SIGHT WORDS

Write the letters on the lines to spell the word <u>again</u>.

1. ___ gain   2. ag ___ n   3. a ___ ___ ___

Name: _____

Author's Purpose WEEK 29 DAY 2

Read the story. Ask yourself, "Why did the author write this story?"

A crab spider looks like a crab.
That's how the crab spider got its name.
A crab spider's body is flat.
Its front legs bend forward.
And it moves sideways.
A crab spider hides in flowers.
That is where it finds bugs to eat.
It has a trick for catching bugs.
A crab spider turns white when it is on a white flower.
It turns yellow when it is on a yellow flower.
The bugs do not see the crab spider.
Zap! The bugs are easy to catch!

Fill in the circle next to the correct answer.

1. Why did the author write the story?
   - Ⓐ to make you laugh
   - Ⓑ to make you afraid of spiders
   - Ⓒ to tell you about crab spiders

2. What does the author tell you about crab spiders?
   - Ⓐ They live in water.
   - Ⓑ They build webs to catch bugs.
   - Ⓒ They can change colors.

3. Why does the author tell what a crab spider looks like?
   - Ⓐ to tell how the spider catches bugs
   - Ⓑ to tell how the spider got its name
   - Ⓒ to tell how big the spider is

SIGHT WORDS

Circle the word that correctly completes the sentence.

(Where   When) did James leave the party?

Name: _____

Author's Purpose — WEEK 29 DAY 3

Read the story. Ask yourself, "Why did the author write this story?"

An itsy-bitsy bug flew up to Hare.
"Will you play with me?" asked Bug.
"I'm too big to play with you," said Hare.
And he hopped away while singing a song.
Hare's singing woke Bear from a long nap.
"You will be my yummy snack!" growled Bear.
He grabbed Hare by his long ears.
"P-p-please don't eat me!" cried Hare.
Just then, Bug buzzed by and tickled Bear's nose.
Bear let go of Hare and swung his paws at Bug.
"Get away, you pest!" yelled Bear.
"Okay!" said Bug. And Hare and Bug got away.

Fill in the circle next to the correct answer.

1. The author wrote the story _____.
   Ⓐ so you will stay away from bears
   Ⓑ to teach you about bugs
   Ⓒ for you to enjoy

2. What makes the story make-believe?
   Ⓐ Animals talk like people.
   Ⓑ A bug is a pest.
   Ⓒ A bear growls.

3. The story belongs in a book _____.
   Ⓐ of true stories
   Ⓑ of folk tales
   Ⓒ about wild animals

SIGHT WORDS

Circle the two words that are the same.

1. ate   2. ask   3. any   4. as   5. ask

Name: _____

Author's Purpose WEEK 29 DAY 4

Read the story. Ask yourself, "Why did the author write this story?"

Baby skunks are called kits.
Newborn kits drink milk from their mother.
Their ears and eyes are closed.
And they have just a little fur.
So their mother keeps them safe and warm.
Kits change as the weeks go by.
They can see and hear, so they can play together.
Their fur is longer, too.
Kits can do more when they are eight weeks old.
They go on short walks with their mother.
And they eat flowers and leaves.
A few months later, the kits will be grown up.

Fill in the circle next to the correct answer.

1. Why did the author write this story?
   Ⓐ to tell you to stay away from skunks
   Ⓑ to tell you what to feed skunks
   Ⓒ to tell you about baby skunks

2. Which fact tells about newborn kits?
   Ⓐ They play together.
   Ⓑ They drink milk from their mother.
   Ⓒ They go on short walks.

3. When the author writes about **kits,** the author is telling about _____.
   Ⓐ all baby animals
   Ⓑ grown-up skunks
   Ⓒ baby skunks

SIGHT WORDS

Circle the word that correctly completes the sentence.

There were (eat   eight) candles on the cake.

Name: _____

Author's Purpose   WEEK 29 DAY 5

Read the story. Ask yourself, "Why did the author write this story?"

Eric Carle writes books for children.
Mr. Carle likes walking in the woods.
So he often writes about animals.
The animals in his books are like people.
A caterpillar is hungry, and a firefly is lonely.
A ladybug is grouchy, and a cat is lost.
Mr. Carle often makes the pictures for his books.
He uses thin colored paper.
He places one color on top of another.
Take a look at some of Eric Carle's books.
You will see a happy sun in almost every book.

Fill in the circle next to the correct answer.

1. The author wrote the story _____.
   Ⓐ to show you how to write a book
   Ⓑ to tell you about a real person
   Ⓒ to laugh at the grouchy ladybug

2. Who is Eric Carle?
   Ⓐ a child who writes books
   Ⓑ a man who likes bugs
   Ⓒ a man who writes books for children

3. In the story, you learn that _____.
   Ⓐ Eric Carle likes cats the best
   Ⓑ Eric Carle makes pictures out of paper
   Ⓒ Eric Carle writes books for grown-ups

SIGHT WORDS

Circle the two words that are the same.

1. take   2. thank   3. make   4. made   5. take

WEEK 30

Prediction

With Prediction, students use clues from a story and prior knowledge to predict what will happen next. Students understand that good predictions follow logically from the events of the story.

DAY 1

Tell students that this week they will practice the reading skill of *Prediction.* Say: **To *predict* means to make a good guess about what may happen next. Good readers pay attention to what story characters say and do. They use these clues to predict what will happen next.** Read the instructions at the top of the page aloud. Then ask students to read the story with you. After reading, allow time for students to complete the activities. Then check their responses for the first activity. Have students support their answers by referring to specific actions of the characters in the story. For the word meanings activity, ask students to read aloud the sentence in the story that uses the word *shoos.* Ask: **What clues does the sentence give to help you figure out the correct answer?**

DAY 2

Review the skill by recalling the prediction made about the family in the story for Day 1. (They will eat a meal.) Ask students to recall the actions that are clues to making the prediction. (e.g., Meatloaf is baking. The table is being set. Milk is being poured.) Then read the instructions. Say: **Today we will make a prediction about a girl named Emma. Her actions are clues to what will happen next.** Have students read the story with you. After reading, answer item 1 in the first activity together. Then have students work alone or with a partner to circle the clues in the story that helped them make that prediction. (all of Emma's actions in setting up her stand) Go over students' responses. Then let students complete the page.

DAY 3

Remind students of the skill. Then say: **Today's story is about a cat named Coco. To make a prediction, pay close attention to Coco's actions. If you know about cats, you can also use what you know to help you predict what will happen next.** Read the instructions aloud, and then have students read the story with you. Allow them time to complete the first activity. Encourage students to refer to the story or their experiences to support their answer choices. Instruct students to do the word meanings activity independently. Check the activities together.

DAY 4

Say: **Today we will read a nonfiction story about honeybees. You will make predictions about what the bees will do next. What clues can you look for in the story?** (the actions of the bees) Read the instructions aloud and have students read the story with you. You may wish to read it a second time to increase comprehension. Instruct students to complete the first activity independently. Check their responses, clarifying any misconceptions by referring to the facts in the story. Have students do the word meanings activity alone or with a partner. Ask students to tell a partner what the word *wag* means. (go back and forth)

DAY 5

Tell students that today's story is about a dog named Homer. Say: **Pay attention to Homer's actions, because they are clues that will help you make predictions. You can also use what you know about dogs to predict what will happen next.** Read the instructions aloud. Then invite students to read the story with you. After reading, let them complete the activities independently. Check their responses. Encourage students to use story details to support their answer choices.

Name: _____

Prediction WEEK 30 DAY 1

Read the story. Ask yourself, "What will the family probably do next?"

The kitchen smells good.
Meatloaf is baking in the oven.
Dia is setting the table.
She likes to make the forks and knives even.
Daniel pours milk into two glasses.
His cat sees the milk and hops onto the table.
Daniel shoos away his cat with his hand.
Dad whistles as he slices the bread.
He places the bread in a basket.
Then Mom hurries into the room.
She's a little late from work.
"I'll make a salad," says Mom.

Fill in the circle next to the correct answer.

1. What will the family probably do next?
   Ⓐ They will go to bed.
   Ⓑ They will eat a meal.
   Ⓒ They will play a game.

2. What will the cat try to do?
   Ⓐ drink the milk
   Ⓑ grab a piece of bread
   Ⓒ help set the table

3. Which sentence best describes the family?
   Ⓐ They work together.
   Ⓑ They are in a hurry.
   Ⓒ They are late.

WORD MEANINGS

Circle the word that correctly completes the sentence.

Tim (shoos   shoes) flies away from his face.

Name: _____

WEEK 30
Prediction DAY 2

Read the story. Ask yourself, "What will the girl probably do next?"

The day is sunny, which is perfect for Emma.
She pulls a small table to the sidewalk.
She brings a chair, too.
Emma covers the table with a cloth.
Then she carefully places a big pitcher on it.
She does not want the lemonade to spill.
Emma stacks some paper cups.
She puts a sign where everyone can see it.
Finally, Emma checks her small box.
There is enough money to make change.

Fill in the circle next to the correct answer.

1. What will Emma probably do?
   Ⓐ sell the table
   Ⓑ sell lemonade
   Ⓒ sell paper cups

2. What might the sign say?
   Ⓐ "Free Lemonade"
   Ⓑ "Paper Cups 5¢ each"
   Ⓒ "Lemonade 10¢ a cup"

3. How do you know that Emma wants to sell something?
   Ⓐ She has money to make change.
   Ⓑ She puts a chair by the table.
   Ⓒ She stacks a pile of paper cups.

WORD MEANINGS

Emma has money to make change.
Circle what it means to "make change."

   1. to give back money   2. to become a different color

Name: _____

Prediction WEEK 30 DAY 3

Read the story. Ask yourself, "What will probably happen next?"

Coco the cat does not like her cat carrier.
She cries whenever she is put inside.
John must take Coco to the vet.
He needs to get his cat into the carrier.
John has a plan for tricking Coco.
When it is time to leave, John calls her.
He gives her a few cat treats to eat.
Then he quickly grabs Coco.
He holds her close.
John carries her to another room.
That is where he keeps the cat carrier.
John opens the door.
Uh-oh! Coco sees the carrier.

Fill in the circle next to the correct answer.

1. What will probably happen next?
   Ⓐ Coco will walk into the cat carrier.
   Ⓑ Coco will lick John's face.
   Ⓒ Coco will try to get away.

2. Which one is part of John's plan?
   Ⓐ He uses treats to get Coco.
   Ⓑ He keeps Coco outside.
   Ⓒ He covers Coco with a cloth.

3. Which one would be best for John to do the next time he has to put Coco in the cat carrier?
   Ⓐ get someone to help
   Ⓑ put a mask on Coco
   Ⓒ put Coco in a sheet

WORD MEANINGS

John tries to trick Coco. Circle what it means to "trick."

1. to fool someone
2. to make something go away

Name: _____

Prediction WEEK 30 DAY 4

Read the story. Ask yourself, "What will probably happen next?"

This honeybee is working hard.
It flies from flower to flower to flower.
It sucks sweet liquid called nectar.
Then the bee flies back to its hive.
The other bees will turn the nectar into honey.
But first they wait for the honeybee to dance.
The dance will tell where to find the best flowers.
The honeybee might do a circle dance.
That means the best flowers are nearby.
Or the bee might wag its body.
That dance means the flowers are farther away.
This time the honeybee dances in a circle.

Fill in the circle next to the correct answer.

1. What will the bees probably do next?
   Ⓐ fly to flowers that are far away
   Ⓑ fly to flowers that are close by
   Ⓒ shout "Hooray!"

2. Why do honeybees suck nectar?
   Ⓐ Nectar helps them dance.
   Ⓑ They use nectar to make honey.
   Ⓒ Nectar makes them strong.

3. What will a honeybee probably do when it finds good flowers far from the hive?
   Ⓐ It will stamp its feet.
   Ⓑ It will do a circle dance.
   Ⓒ It will wag its body.

WORD MEANINGS

Write yes on the line if the thing can wag. Write no if it cannot wag.

1. a dog's tail _____   2. a page in a book _____

Name: _____

Prediction WEEK 30 DAY 5

Read the story. Ask yourself, "What will probably happen next?"

Homer the puppy loves to eat.
He will eat almost anything.
He chews grass and bugs.
He gnaws on shoes and dolls.
Homer even eats ears of corn.
He puts his paws on the corn to hold it still.
The kitchen is Homer's favorite room.
He likes sitting under the baby's chair.
The baby is learning how to eat.
Often, the baby drops her food.

Fill in the circle next to the correct answer.

1. What will probably happen to the food the baby drops?
   Ⓐ Homer will eat the food.
   Ⓑ Homer will give back the food.
   Ⓒ Homer will leave the food alone.

2. What would Homer probably do at a picnic?
   Ⓐ stay away from the food
   Ⓑ sleep while people eat
   Ⓒ sit under the picnic table

3. Which sentence tells why Homer sits under the chair?
   Ⓐ "The kitchen is Homer's favorite room."
   Ⓑ "Often, the baby drops her food."
   Ⓒ "Homer even eats ears of corn."

WORD MEANINGS

Circle two words in the story that are ways to eat.

© Evan-Moor Corp. • EMC 3451 • Daily Reading Comprehension

Answer Key

WEEK 1

DAY 1
1. A 2. C 3. B
Beginning Sounds   but

DAY 2
1. C 2. B 3. A
Vowel Sounds   have

DAY 3
1. A 2. B 3. B
Rhyming Words
my, sky, fly

DAY 4
1. B 2. C 3. A
Beginning Sounds   feed

DAY 5
1. A 2. C 3. C
Beginning Sounds (any two)
mop, my, me, mud

WEEK 2

DAY 1
1. A 2. C 3. B
Sight Words   good

DAY 2
1. C 2. B 3. A
Sight Words   has

DAY 3
1. C 2. B 3. A
Sight Words   two

DAY 4
1. B 2. B 3. C
Sight Words   are

DAY 5
1. C 2. A 3. A
Sight Words   not

WEEK 3

DAY 1
1. A 2. C 3. A
Word Meanings

DAY 2
1. A 2. C 3. B
Word Meanings

DAY 3
1. B 2. A 3. B
Word Meanings   finally

DAY 4
1. B 2. C 3. C
Word Meanings   soon

DAY 5
1. A 2. C 3. C
Word Meanings   a cotton ball

WEEK 4

DAY 1
1. B 2. B 3. B
Rhyming Words
wear, their

DAY 2
1. C 2. A 3. C
Ending Sounds
big, dog, tug

DAY 3
1. B 2. C 3. A
Vowel Sounds   sky

DAY 4
1. C 2. B 3. C
Vowel Sounds   shop

DAY 5
1. A 2. A 3. C
Vowel Sounds   beak

WEEK 5

DAY 1
1. C 2. A 3. A
Sight Words   said

DAY 2
1. A 2. C 3. B
Sight Words   soon

DAY 3
1. C 2. C 3. B
Sight Words   ride

DAY 4
1. A 2. C 3. A
Sight Words
1. pl   2. se   3. ea

DAY 5
1. A 2. A 3. C
Sight Words   her

WEEK 6

DAY 1
1. C 2. C 3. B
Word Meanings

DAY 2
1. A 2. A 3. A
Word Meanings
1. cluck   2. peep

DAY 3
1. A 2. C 3. C
Word Meanings   to get

DAY 4
1. C 2. B 3. A
Word Meanings
Answers will vary—
e.g., glue

DAY 5
1. C 2. A 3. B
Word Meanings

WEEK 7

DAY 1
1. B 2. C 3. B
Beginning Sounds
1. Big Bear   2. Pig's Pies

DAY 2
1. B 2. C 3. C
Beginning Sounds (any two)
tiny, tall, tree, to, too

DAY 3
1. C 2. B 3. A
Vowel Sounds   icy

DAY 4
1. B 2. A 3. C
Beginning Sounds (any two)
were, with, wash,
washed, wet, was

DAY 5
1. B 2. A 3. A
Ending Sounds
sun, can, burn

WEEK 8

DAY 1
1. C 2. C 3. A
Sight Words   then

DAY 2
1. A 2. B 3. A
Sight Words   use

DAY 3
1. B 2. C 3. C
Sight Words   his

DAY 4
1. C 2. A 3. C
Sight Words   put

DAY 5
1. C 2. C 3. A
Sight Words   eat

WEEK 9

DAY 1
1. C 2. A 3. B
Word Meanings

DAY 2
1. A 2. B 3. C
Word Meanings

WEEK 10

DAY 3
1. C 2. A 3. A
Word Meanings

DAY 4
1. B 2. C 3. A
Word Meanings
in the morning,
at night, in the afternoon

DAY 5
1. A 2. C 3. B
Word Meanings
to come out of an egg

WEEK 10

DAY 1
1. C 2. C 3. A
Beginning Sounds
1. s   2. k

DAY 2
1. B 2. A 3. B
Vowel Sounds
peel, tree, eat, seed

DAY 3
1. B 2. A 3. A
Vowel Sounds
dry, sky

DAY 4
1. A 2. C 3. B
Ending Sounds
things, reads, animals,
spiders, friends, stretches

DAY 5
1. B 2. C 3. B
Ending Sounds
birds, feathers,
chickens, webs

WEEK 11

DAY 1
1. B 2. A 3. B
Sight Words
1. e   2. w   3. r   4. ere

DAY 2
1. C 2. B 3. B
Sight Words   was

DAY 3
1. B 2. A 3. C
Sight Words   that

DAY 4
1. A 2. C 3. A
Sight Words
1. e   2. wh   3. here

DAY 5
1. C 2. B 3. C
Sight Words   They

WEEK 12

DAY 1
1. B 2. C 3. B
Word Meanings

DAY 2
1. C 2. B 3. A
Word Meanings
1.
2.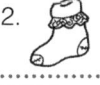

DAY 3
1. A 2. C 3. B
Word Meanings
pennies, books

DAY 4
1. C 2. A 3. C
Word Meanings

DAY 5
1. B 2. C 3. A
Word Meanings   all

WEEK 13

DAY 1
1. A 2. C 3. B
Rhyming Words
sea, tree; sky, fly

DAY 2
1. C 2. C 3. B
Vowel Sounds
soon, room

DAY 3
1. B 2. C 3. A
Beginning Sounds
1. **sh**eep   3. **wh**ile
2. **th**em

DAY 4
1. A 2. B 3. C
Rhyming Words
snake, lake

DAY 5
1. A 2. A 3. C
Vowel Sounds
1. b**e**   3. f**ee**t   5. part**y**
2. thr**ee** 4. **ea**t

WEEK 14

DAY 1
1. C 2. B 3. B
Sight Words
1. der 2. un 3. er

DAY 2
1. B 2. C 3. A
Sight Words
1. c 2. ld 3. ou

DAY 3
1. C 2. B 3. B
Sight Words   went

DAY 4
1. A 2. B 3. B
Sight Words   must

DAY 5
1. C 2. B 3. A
Sight Words   live

WEEK 15

DAY 1
1. B 2. A 3. C
Word Meanings   clay

DAY 2
1. A 2. A 3. A
Word Meanings (any three)
tugs, rubs, takes, wiggles, stands, stares

DAY 3
1. C 2. B 3. A
Word Meanings
to fall out

DAY 4
1. A 2. B 3. B
Word Meanings   gills

DAY 5
1. B 2. A 3. A
Word Meanings
The cat ran.

WEEK 16

DAY 1
1. C 2. B 3. A
Compound Words
1. class|room
2. hand|writing
3. every|one

DAY 2
1. C 2. A 3. B
Rhyming Words
Answers will vary.

DAY 3
1. A 2. C 3. C
Vowel Sounds
around, mouth

DAY 4
1. C 2. B 3. A
Vowel Sounds
1. ī 2. ē 3. ē

DAY 5
1. A 2. B 3. B
Vowel Sounds
catch, bat, basket

WEEK 17

DAY 1
1. A 2. C 3. A
Sight Words   with

DAY 2
1. C 2. B 3. C
Sight Words   of

DAY 3
1. A 2. B 3. C
Sight Words
1. j 2. us 3. u, t

DAY 4
1. B 2. B 3. C
Sight Words   like

DAY 5
1. B 2. A 3. A
Sight Words   every

WEEK 18

DAY 1
1. A 2. A 3. C
Word Meanings
Dad shakes Sparky's leash.

DAY 2
1. B 2. A 3. B
Word Meanings

DAY 3
1. C 2. B 3. A
Word Meanings
to save

DAY 4
1. C 2. C 3. A
Word Meanings

DAY 5
1. B 2. A 3. C
Word Meanings
a big truck, thunder

WEEK 19

DAY 1
1. C 2. B 3. C
Vowel Sounds
g**oa**t, m**ow**, t**oe**, sl**ow**

DAY 2
1. B 2. C 3. A
Vowel Sounds
1. tape   3. cute
2. made   4. plane

DAY 3
1. A 2. C 3. B
Consonant Sounds
1. g 2. j 3. g

DAY 4
1. C 2. B 3. A
Vowel Sounds
ceiling, creatures, sleep, leave, deep

DAY 5
1. C 2. C 3. B
Rhyming Words
dare, there, air, stare

WEEK 20

DAY 1
1. B 2. C 3. C
Sight Words   out

DAY 2
1. A 2. C 3. B
Sight Words   one

DAY 3
1. C 2. B 3. A
Sight Words
1. here 2. th 3. er

DAY 4
1. C 2. C 3. A
Sight Words   know

DAY 5
1. A 2. A 3. B
Sight Words   from

WEEK 21

DAY 1
1. B 2. A 3. A
Word Meanings   set

DAY 2
1. A 2. A 3. B
Word Meanings   circle

DAY 3
1. B 2. C 3. C
Word Meanings   tugged

DAY 4
1. C 2. A 3. B
Word Meanings
on the face

DAY 5
1. B 2. A 3. B
Word Meanings
1.

WEEK 22

DAY 1
1. C 2. A 3. C
Vowel Sounds
groups, cool

DAY 2
1. C 2. B 3. C
Vowel Sounds
1. tr**ea**t   3. cr**ea**m
2. cook**ie**   4. p**ie**ce

DAY 3
1. C 2. A 3. B
Long Vowel Sounds
sheep, people, eat, cheese, curly

DAY 4
1. A 2. B 3. B
Vowel Sounds
1. a   2. i   3. e

DAY 5
1. B 2. B 3. C
Ending Sounds
1. z   2. s

WEEK 23

DAY 1
1. B 2. C 3. C
Sight Words   over

DAY 2
1. B 2. C 3. C
Sight Words
1. ou   2. ough   3. throu

DAY 3
1. A 2. A 3. C
Sight Words   let

DAY 4
1. B 2. A 3. C
Sight Words
1. wh   2. ite   3. e

DAY 5
1. B 2. B 3. B
Sight Words   have

WEEK 24

DAY 1
1. A 2. C 3. B
Word Meanings
tore, snipped, tugged, plucked

DAY 2
1. C 2. A 3. A
Word Meanings
Answers will vary.

DAY 3
1. B 2. C 3. C
Word Meanings
whooshed, zipped, zoomed

DAY 4
1. A 2. C 3. B
Word Meanings
Answers will vary.

DAY 5
1. B 2. A 3. B
Word Meanings
The stairs squeaked.

WEEK 25

DAY 1
1. B 2. C 3. A
Rhyming Words
you, do; stars, Mars; cream, team

DAY 2
1. B 2. C 3. A
Vowel Sounds
Be sure students read accurately.

DAY 3
1. C 2. B 3. C
Base Words and Endings
1. flash**ed**   3. say**s**
2. spoil**ing**   4. walk**ed**

DAY 4
1. B 2. C 3. A
Consonant Sounds
1. **sm**all   3. **st**ick
2. **sk**in   4. **sp**ot

DAY 5
1. B 2. A 3. B
Syllables
1. 2   2. 2   3. 1   4. 1

WEEK 26

DAY 1
1. C 2. B 3. C
Sight Words   saw

DAY 2
1. C 2. A 3. B
Sight Words   walk

DAY 3
1. A 2. C 3. A
Sight Words
1. ter   2. a, r   3. ter

DAY 4
1. A 2. A 3. B
Sight Words   this

DAY 5
1. B 2. A 3. B
Sight Words   old

WEEK 27

DAY 1
1. B 2. C 3. A
Word Meanings
makes the dirt flat

DAY 2
1. C 2. A 3. B
Word Meanings
Answers will vary.

DAY 3
1. C 2. A 3. B
Word Meanings   middle

DAY 4
1. A 2. B 3. C
Word Meanings
to get milk out of a cow

DAY 5
1. A 2. C 3. A
Word Meanings
in the ocean

WEEK 28

DAY 1
1. B 2. A 3. A
Blends
1. **sw**eater   3. **sm**all
2. **st**ore   4. **sk**ip

DAY 2
1. C 2. A 3. C
Plural Words
butterflies, moths, wings, flowers

DAY 3
1. B 2. C 3. B
Syllables
1. but|ter   3. ap|ple
2. car|rots

DAY 4
1. B 2. B 3. C
Vowel Sounds
1. st**oo**d   3. f**oo**t
2. c**ou**ld

DAY 5
1. A 2. B 3. A
Long Vowel Sounds
fairy, very, scary

WEEK 29

DAY 1
1. A 2. B 3. B
Sight Words
1. a   2. ai   3. gain

DAY 2
1. C 2. C 3. B
Sight Words   When

DAY 3
1. C 2. A 3. B
Sight Words   ask

DAY 4
1. C 2. B 3. C
Sight Words   eight

DAY 5
1. B 2. C 3. B
Sight Words   take

WEEK 30

DAY 1
1. B 2. A 3. A
Word Meanings   shoos

DAY 2
1. B 2. C 3. A
Word Meanings
to give back money

DAY 3
1. C 2. A 3. A
Word Meanings
to fool someone

DAY 4
1. B 2. B 3. C
Word Meanings
1. yes   2. no

DAY 5
1. A 2. C 3. B
Word Meanings
chews, gnaws